**STARMAP
SCORPIO**

SCORPIO
DISCOVER A NEW YOU

RYUJI KAGAMI

ONE PEACE BOOKS

There is a deep, deep well at the bottom of your heart.
It is filled to the brim with clear, clean water.

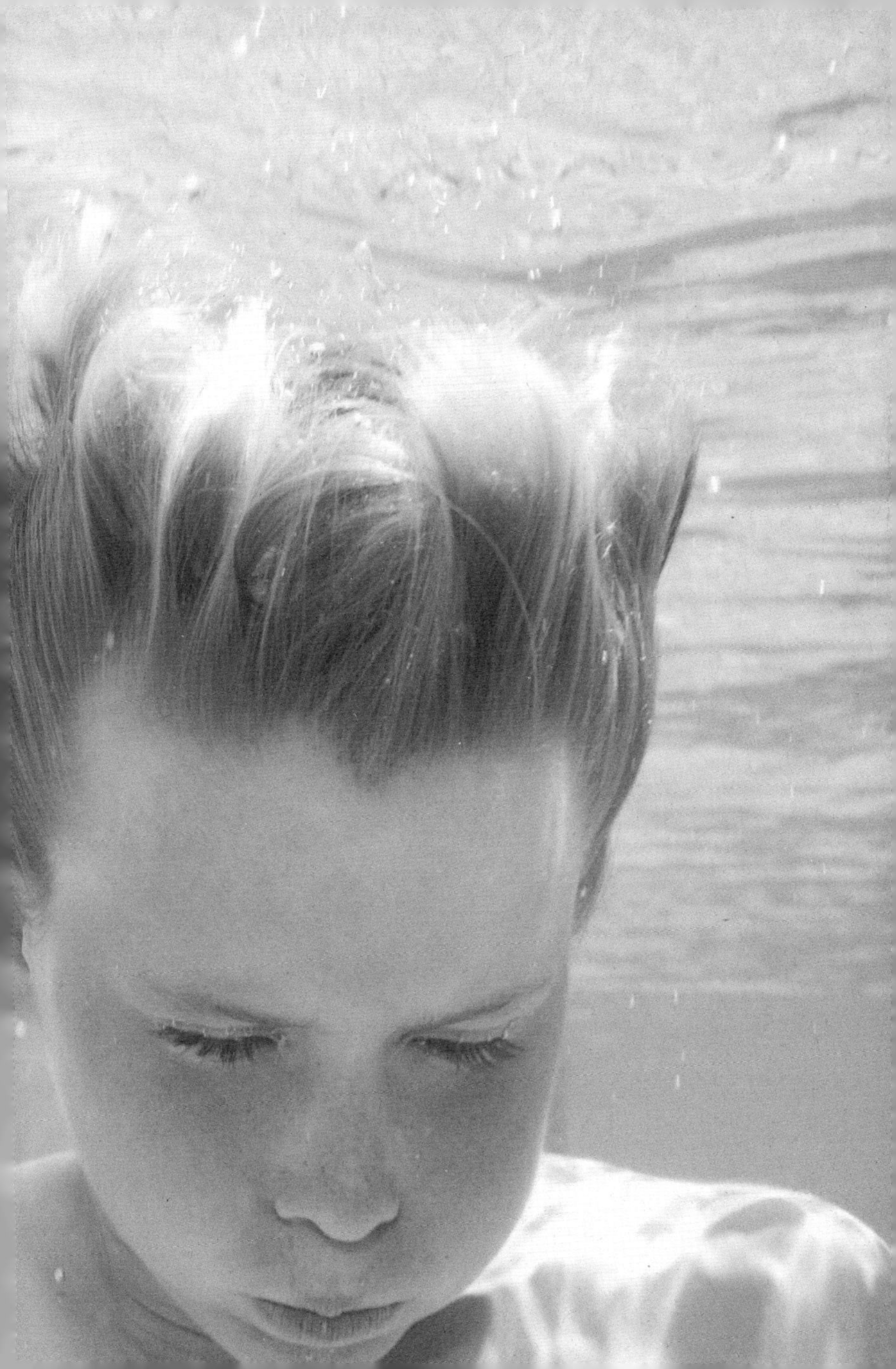

Scorpios love more, fall in love more, than anyone else.

When a Scorpio says they "like" something, the word means more than when others say the same thing. It means so much it causes the heart to quake. They mean it so much it causes the self to disintegrate.

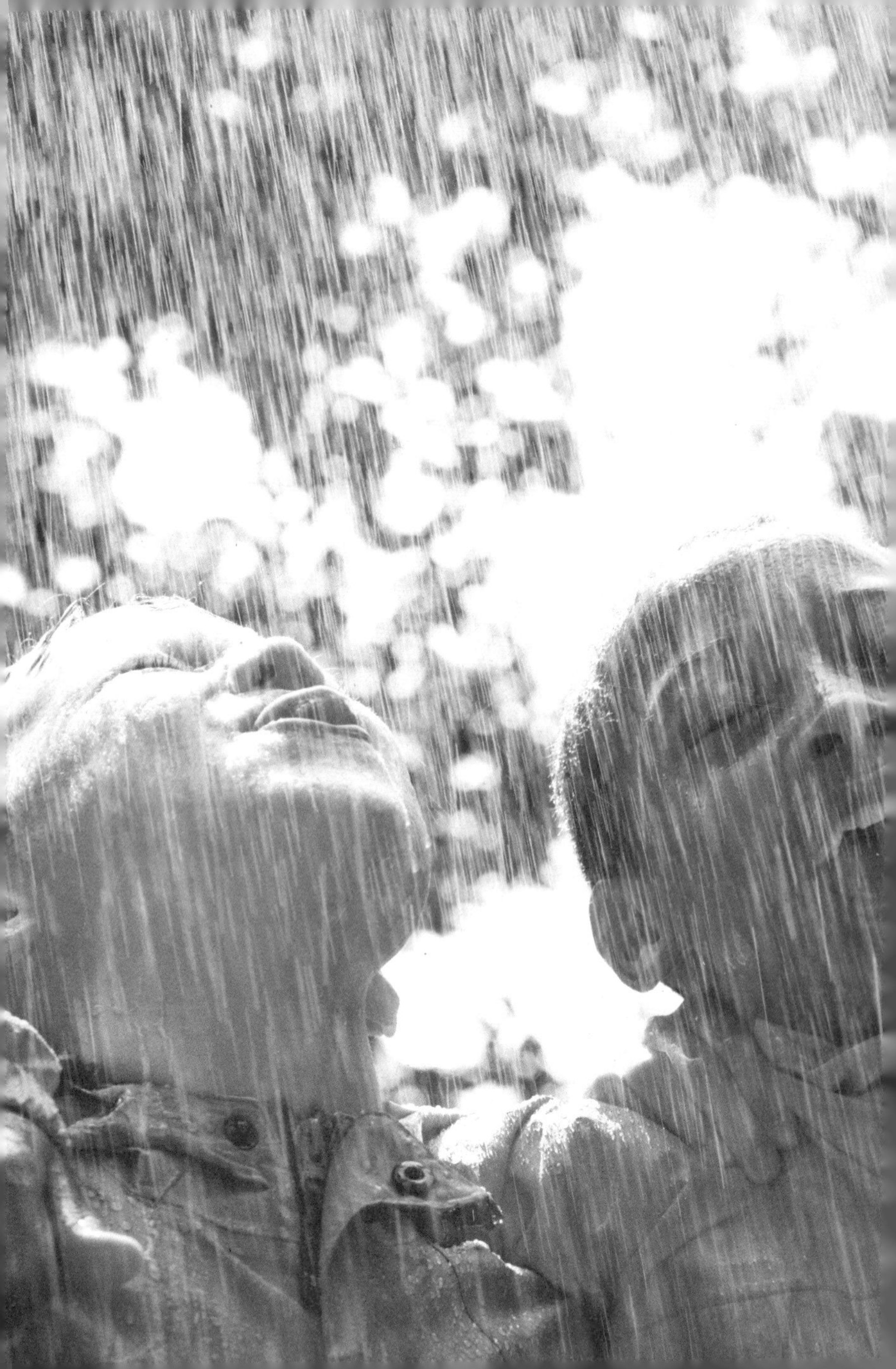

No matter the strength of the coming storm, the size of the sweeping wave, the height of the wall, there is nothing to fear. The hardest times are always new beginnings for Scorpios.

There once was a boy who said the beauty of the desert is its secret stores of water. Look inside yourself for that well. Dig it out. Sink as deeply as you can. The answers you seek are at the bottom.

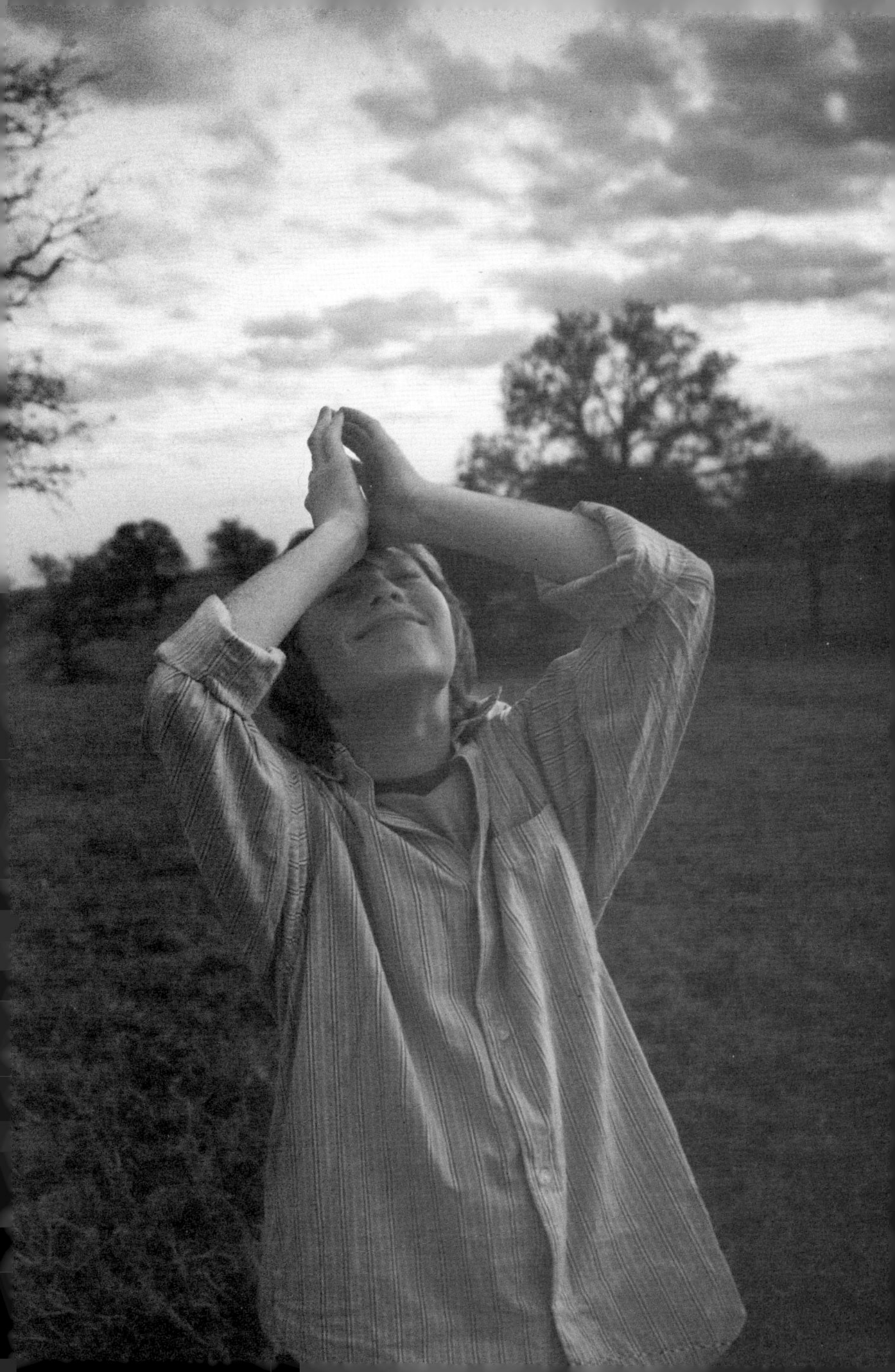

You see to the depths of all things. Inside and outside, Good and Evil, yourself and others. You can pass over any border.
You don't have to be a "good" person. You don't need the understanding of others. There's no need to flatter others. Nothing suits you less than "faking it."

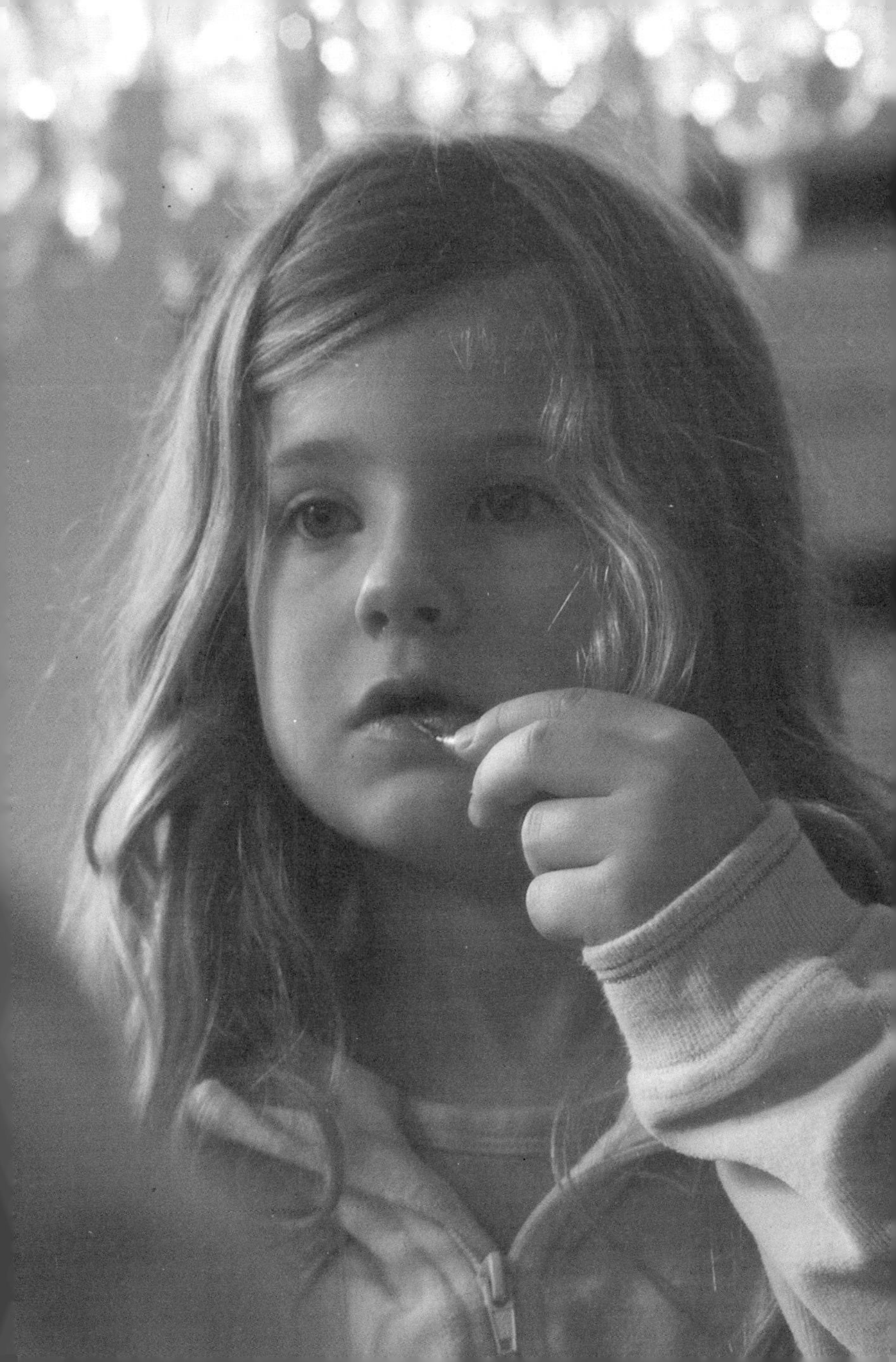

It's okay to fail.

It's okay to lose.

It's okay to be wrong.

But,

fail completely.

Lose completely.

Be completely wrong.

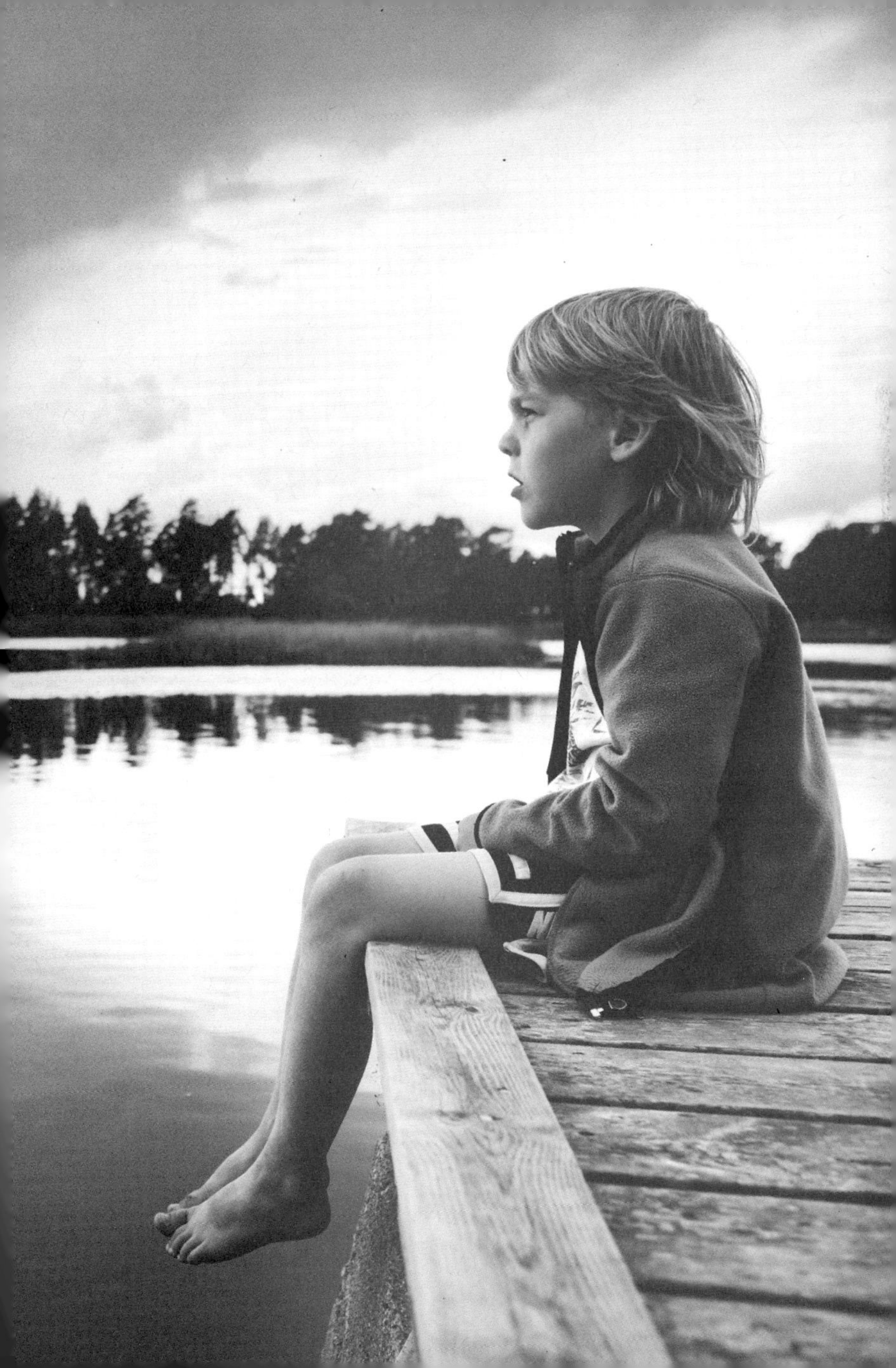

Give yourself completely to what you do.

Do everything the best you can.

A new you is waiting on the other side of all of it.

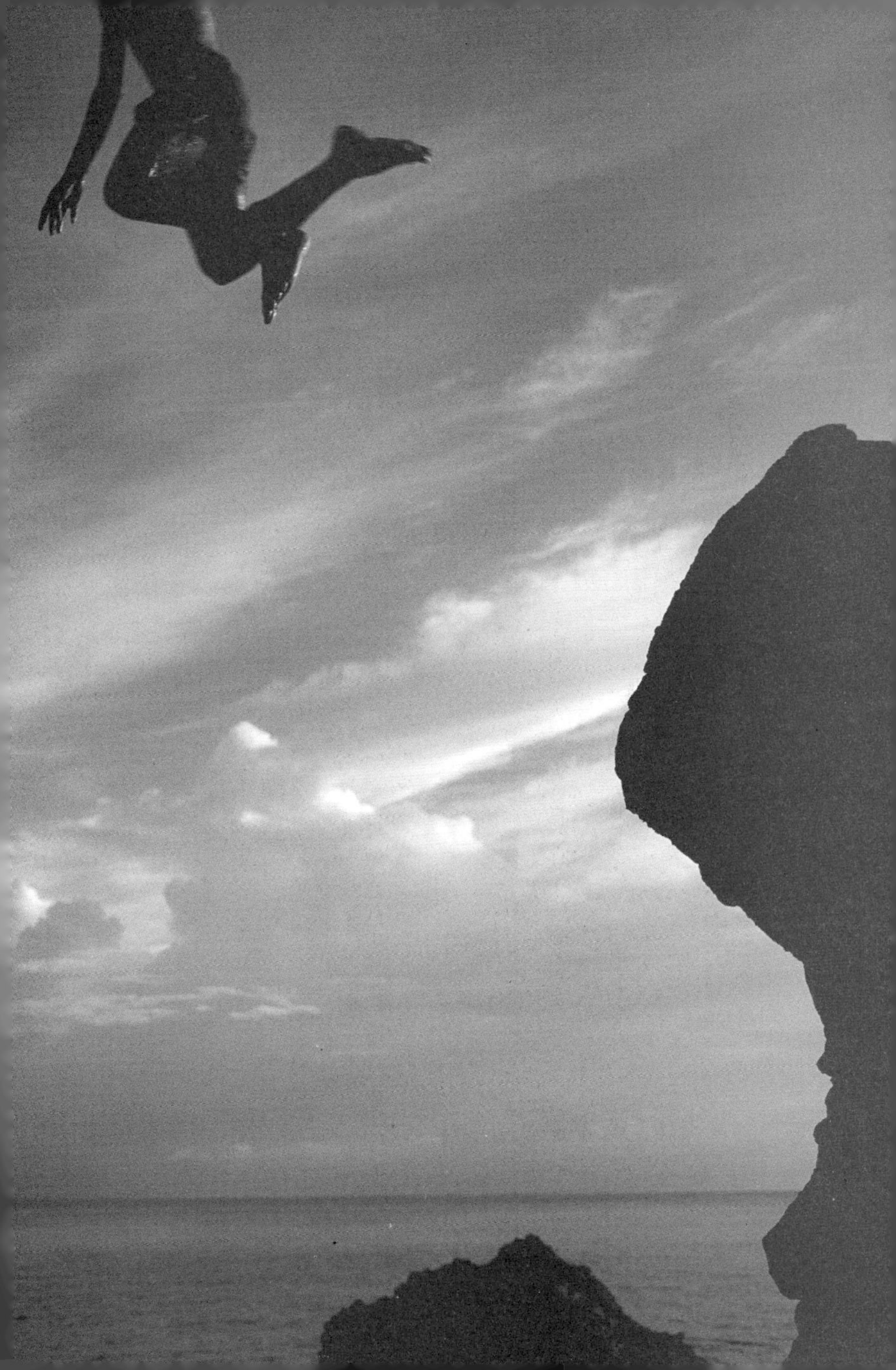

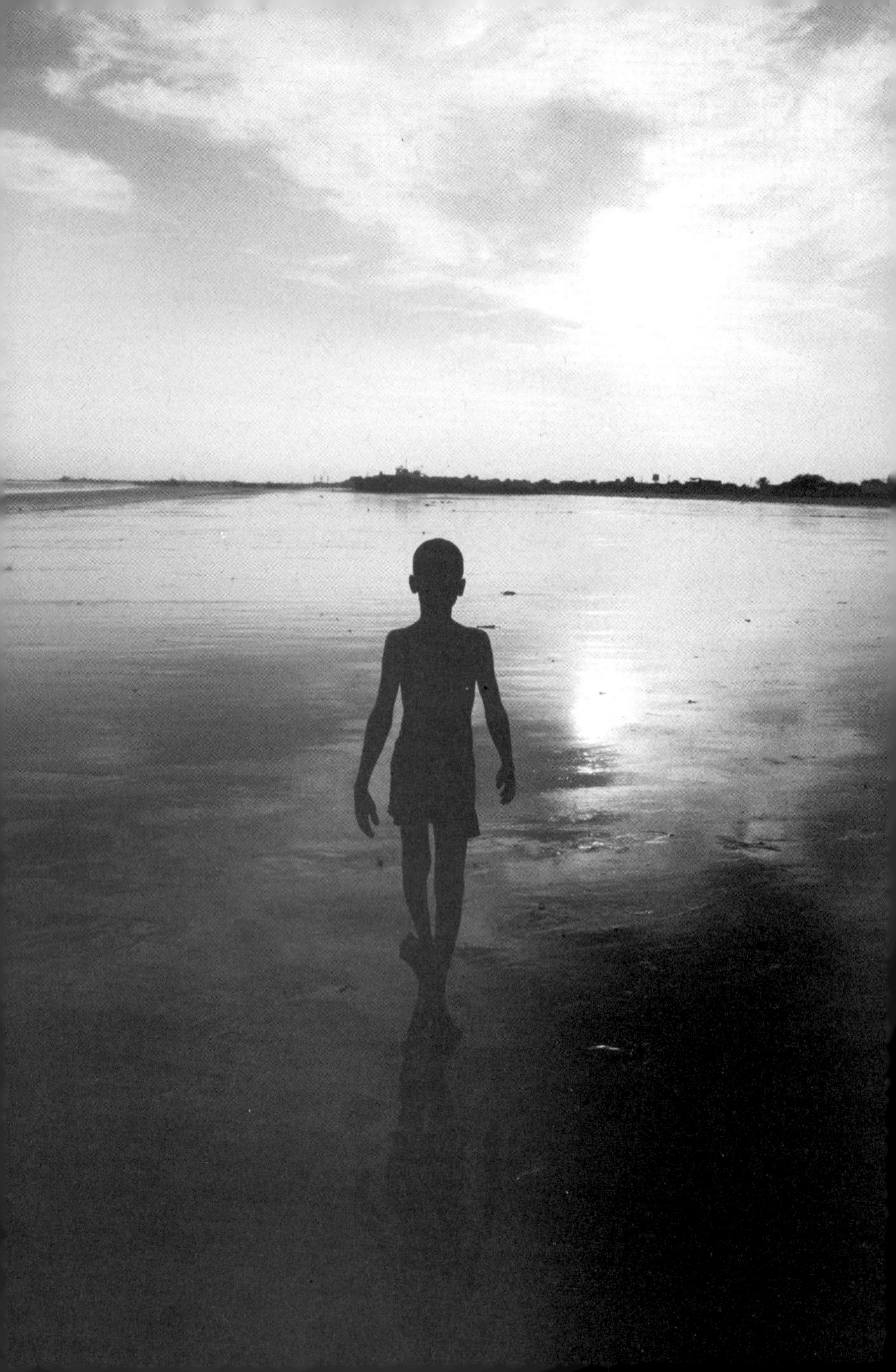

Scorpios love more than others, love deeper than others.

The simple, superficial emotions of others mean little to Scorpios.

Love must be deeper, must be more "real" to satisfy a Scorpio.

They must find something they can love completely. Something they can lose themselves in. Something to devote themselves to.

Once you find those things, there is nothing to fear. No matter the obstacle, tackle it with all your heart and you will overcome it. It is your power to love that carries you across all borders.

Here we deliver 31 messages, to you, Scorpio, to cross all borders and discover your new self.

For you, Scorpio.

That you may live free,

that you may live as yourself.

STARMAP SCORPIO — **CONTENTS**

What do you want to do? Where do you find motivation?

(Dreams / Goals / Motivation) ──────────── 022

Discover your deepest passion.

Listen to your subconscious.

When you're in a tough spot, you can see clearly.

Look for the missing piece.

Savor all you can.

Where can you shine?

(Job / Role / Strengths) ──────────── 034

Work as you love, with all your heart.

Become a specialist in your field.

Hone your presentation skills.

Don't let your hobbies just be hobbies.

Prepare, observe.

What to choose and why.

(Choices / Decisions) ──────────── 048

Focus on what you enjoy.

Give yourself time to think.

Revisit the things you've given up on.

Look for deeper answers and find your true self.

You don't need the answers today.

When you hit a wall, when you hit bottom.

(Adversity / Hard Times) ———————————— 060

    You are strong when you're in a pinch.

    It's okay to fail at something as long as you finish it.

    Let things go.

    Leave revenge to your imagination.

    You don't have to get rid of your negative emotions.

Who will you love?
Who will love you?

(Personal Relationships / Love) ———————————— 074

    Have the courage to take the first step.

    Become someone your partner needs.

    Who should you love?

    Who will really love you?

    Breaking up is not the end, it will bring you new possibilities.

What to value.
How to be yourself.

(Rules / Desires) ———————————— 086

    Flexibility, not flattery.

    Be aware of your own darkness.

    Focus on what you love and cross all borders.

    To be reborn, experience all you can.

    Meeting people will help you meet your dreams.

To live without regret. ———————————— 098

    From "Me" to "Us."

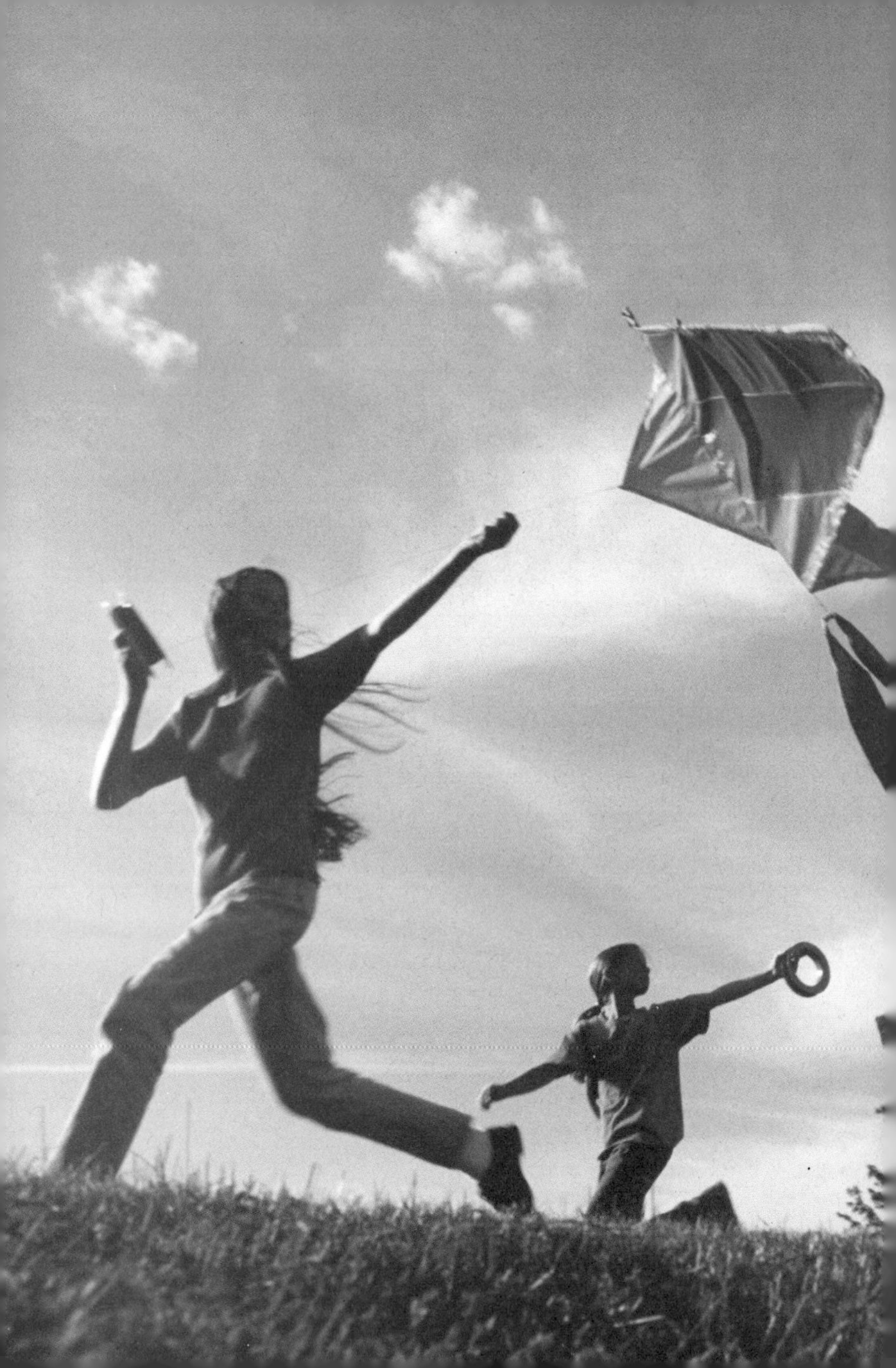

STARMAP SCORPIO

What do you want to do?
Where do you find motivation?

(Dreams / Goals / Motivation)

What is your dream?
What do you do when you lose sight of what you want?
What scares you?
What direction should you take?

STARMAP
SCORPIO

1

Discover your deepest
passion.

The symbol of Scorpio is the scorpion that stung Orion. Perhaps that is why scorpions bring to mind images of poison. Some think of Scorpios as holding onto deep darkness. But these interpretations are not only superficial, they are false. In mythology Orion was a symbol of pride and self-consciousness. When the scorpion killed him, it was to destroy selfish desire and create common good.

Scorpios are known for this very behavior. They shed their skin, put themselves on the line for others, and move us all forward. Therefore, whether it be in matters of work, hobbies, or love, when you get serious and put your mind to it, there is nothing you cannot overcome.

Your amazing ability to concentrate enables you to learn quickly, putting experts to shame in a short amount of time. It enables you to build deep and lasting connections with others. It enables you to climb higher than anyone else. However, simple and shallow emotions fail to move you. Without true, deep stimulation, you are bored. To counter this, make a point to always search out your deepest desires, to encounter fascination, to encounter love.

When you feel drawn to something, go as far as you can. Go to meet the leaders of the field. Don't just read about things, use your body and get out there to actually try them. If you keep stimulating the deepest parts of you heart, you'll find your purpose soon enough. Find your purpose and pursue it. A new you is waiting for you at the end of your journey.

STARMAP
SCORPIO

2

Listen to your subconscious.

Many Scorpios are thought to possess mysterious, spiritual intuitions. It is certainly no coincidence that the protective star of Scorpio is Pluto. In Greek Mythology, Pluto was associated with the unseen world and its ruler, Hades. In psychological terms, it represents Jungian subconsciousness. Because of the influence of Pluto, Scorpios are the most sensitive, most receptive to the whims of the subconscious. They can easily see the emotions and thoughts that others try to hide, and just as easily, they are aware of their own emotions, despite, perhaps, trying to surpress them. Therefore, when it comes time to search out your true calling, there is no need to lend your ear to the thoughts of others.

Don't allow yourself to be swayed by outside information. Just listen to the voice of your subconscious. When it tells you that you've found what you were looking for, believe it! Follow it. If you do, then you will never be wrong about the path you chose, and if you follow it, you are sure to discover a place where you can be yourself and best utilize your talents. Soon enough, you'll come to a future that you never could have imagined, a joy you've never known.

If you find that lately you've been unable to hear that voice, unable to find inspiration in the world, it means that you are surrounded by too much noise, too many distractions from that small voice within. The distractions of a busy life will dull your senses. When you feel that way, take the time to escape from what you know. Go to a town you've never been to. Try yoga, try meditation, try running. It is important to hone your intuition and keep it sharp. Keep yourself in a situation where that is possible. When you hear the voice from within, you've already won the battle.

**STARMAP
SCORPIO**

3

When you're in a tough spot, you can see clearly.

Scorpios have a reputation for tenacity. That doesn't simply mean that you try very hard though, or that you refuse to give up. When Scorpio's fall on hard times, they find their optimism and learn to move forward. When you hit a wall, stores of power well up from within, and new opportunities present themselves. For example, you may run into trouble at work, but in working to recover from your loses, you end up achieving even better things, even larger projects. Or you may be forced to quit your job, but in the process discover what you really want to do. You may get dumped from a long relationship, but discover your true love. You may get sick, but in the process learn to value your health, leading to a more beautiful, healthier you.

It's true, the hard times are filled with possibilities for Scorpios. So when you fall on hard times, look closer and see that that difficulty is simply the start of a path to a new, better you. When you feel unmotivated, try pushing yourself to the limit. If you are unsatisfied with your work, quit your job, and see what happens. If you are unsatisfied in love, break it off and be on your own for a little while. When you simplify your situation, you'll come to see what it is you really wanted all along. That desire of yours, your true desire, will lead you into the future.

STARMAP
SCORPIO

4

Look for the missing piece.

You try and do something, but you have no confidence. Scorpios often drag these negative emotions along with them. Perhaps they were rejected in the past, perhaps they were unable to be satisfied with a past endeavor. Regardless, the problem is not the trauma itself. The problem is that you have shut those emotions away. How, then, are you supposed to move forward?

When you feel held back by negative emotions, look deep into the darkest parts of your heart. When you feel unsatisfied, go on a journey to find what is missing. Face those past experiences that you wish to hide from. This is not to say that doing so will flood your heard with golden light. But if you face your dark past head on, you'll be able to see that those emotions are not the whole of you, they are just a small part.

You don't need to feel worried about those things, you don't even have to solve them. Pick them up and take them with you. For example, if an experience of bullying in the past has made you afraid to put your thoughts out in front of others, that's okay, take however much time you need to dwell on your dream before you chose to divulge it.

Rather, if you find what the missing piece is, why not make it a life goal to fill the gap? Perhaps your father never loved you as a child, and now you look for a father relationship with men. So be it then, find someone who represents an ideal father figure who will love you in the way you need, and heal the wounds of the past. You can bring balance to your life and move on. There is no need to fear the darkness, no need to fear your shortcomings. If you stay positive and look to the future, those very things will bring depth and humanity to your life.

STARMAP
SCORPIO

5

Savor all you can.

When Scorpio finds a goal, or a dream, it is very important that they throw their whole being into it. No matter how deeply you may love something, starting a new project can lead to trepidation. You may feel you stand before a wall. You may also feel that everyone else is moving on, leaving you behind. But that is nothing to worry about. The approval of others and the changing of the times has nothing to do with you. All you need to focus on is your goal, and the processes involved in bringing it to fruition.

If we're talking about work, then just keep going until they fire you. If you run a shop, keep going until the very last customer has left. The same goes for your hobbies. If you like to travel, keep going until you've visited every single place you want to go. If you enjoy comics, continue until you've read every last one. If you keep it up, you'll find yourself in a different place than you started.

Others who understand your desires will appear, and people will appreciate you for your unique perspective. What if you throw your heart into something, and it still doesn't work out? That's fine too. If you do all you can, if you savor the process, then you will have no regrets. Then you can move on to the next project, the next field. Soon you will find success. Once you've set your mind to something, you do the best you can. You don't tolerate mediocrity. That is what make a Scorpio and Scorpio. Search out happiness. If you keep on going until you succeed, it's impossible to fail.

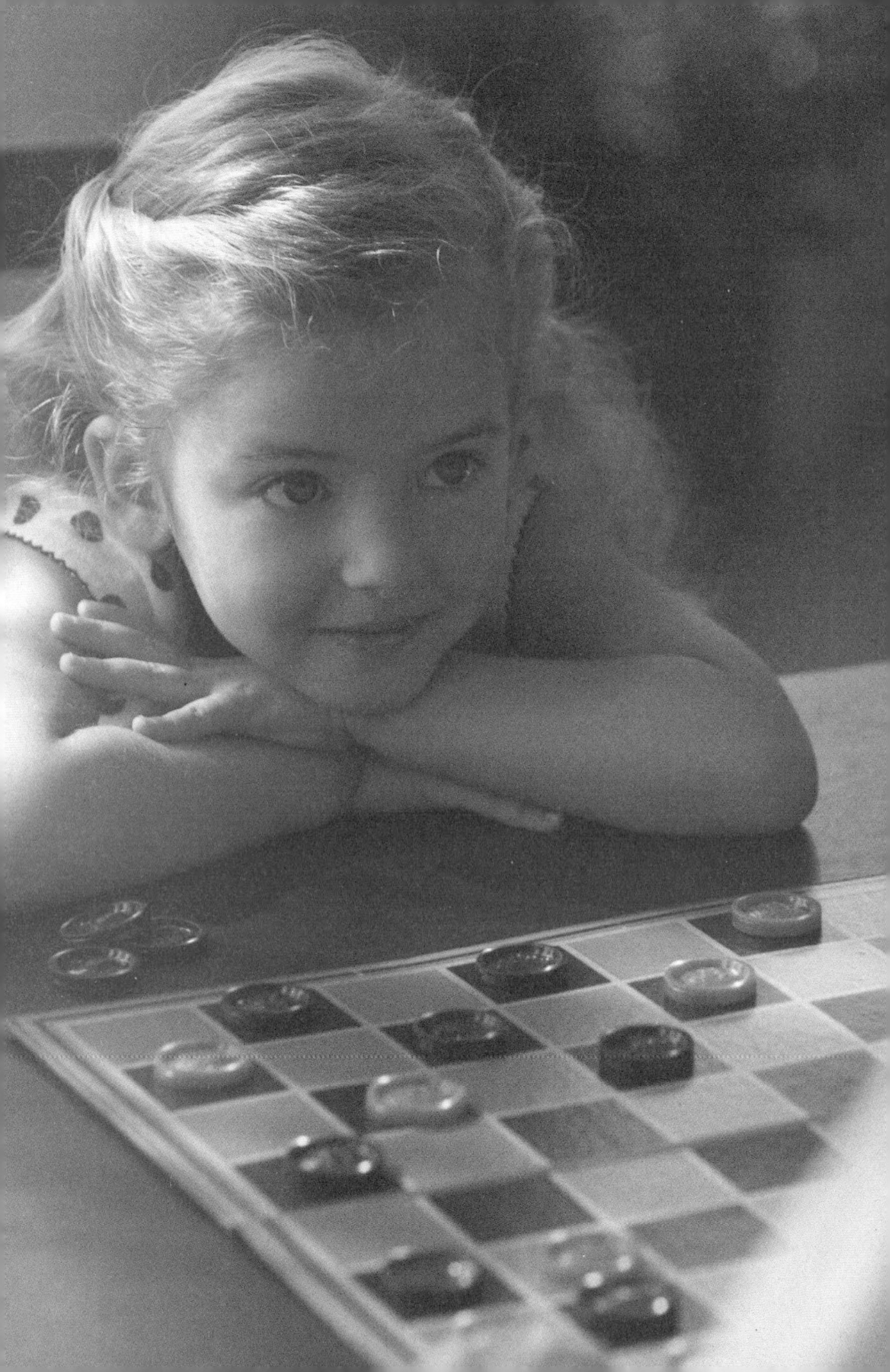

**STARMAP
SCORPIO**

Where can you shine?

(Job / Role / Strengths)

What are you talents?

Where can you best utilize them?

What is your role in the world?

For you, Scorpio, that you may shine your brightest.

STARMAP
SCORPIO

6

Work as you love, with all your heart.

When Scorpio falls in love, they throw themselves into it completely, they give their all to it. It may be that, in love, you may not need to even think about it. But in other matters you become conscious of it, and start to doubt. You start to want a safety net.

You can lose yourself in anything. When a Scorpio gives themselves over completely to something, it is proof that they are alive. Use that energy for your work. Fall in love with your work to the extent that you forget about everything else. Remove the limitations, give your all to it, work with a fire in your belly, and you'll find an ecstasy and catharsis in accomplishing your goals. Allow yourself to be drunk on your work.

There are not many people that can fall in love with their work in this way. If you are not very interested in your actual job, can't you fall in love with the philosophy of your company? Or with the company itself? Can you not feel love for your boss and your employees? When I say "Love your coworkers" I don't mean that you actually need to fall in love with them and pursue a physical relationship. Actually, quite the reverse. If you were to actually fall in love and start a relationship with them, your energies would all flow in that direction, leaving nothing left for your actual job. No, that's not what I mean. I mean to throw your whole being into it, as you do when you are in love with someone. If you keep at it, the resulting community will draw others to you like a magnet. When you allow yourself to be drawn completely into something, you've found the key to success.

STARMAP
SCORPIO

7

Become a specialist in
your field.

Scorpios always throw their entire being into the things they are interested in, the things they love. However, when they find something boring or obnoxious, they lose all motivation. Scorpios are not always able to manage their time well, and when they obsess over one thing, it often leads to the neglect of other, equally important things. They can focus on their jobs completely and perform them excellently, but they are often unable to find balance within their company. This is the reason others often say that Scorpios are unbalanced or biased. But that is just fine. Actually, keep on being biased. Be as biased as you can. Go deeper and deeper into what you care about until you are a specialist in the field. You will become irreplaceable.

If you like to cook, get some qualifications under your belt and become the best cook you can. If you are in accounting, learn a special method of calculation that others simply cannot emulate. If you like books, or clothes, why not work in related retail outlets, or, even better, open your own shop? Your special and unique sense will bring customers to you. If you throw your whole being into it, you really can become an irreplaceable specialist. A balanced journalist can be replaced by anyone. But when you become a journalist, you'll be the only one who can do what you do. You'll be unique.

STARMAP
SCORPIO

8

Hone your presentation skills.

Because you are particular about quality, and because you make that quality your highest priority, you may think that the opinions of others don't matter. But in truth, what you are really after are the feelings of others, the recognition of others. You also have a special ability to recognize the true feelings of others, you can see them even if they are hidden. Therefore, even if you draw the criticism of others, there is no need to alter your plans or projects to suit them. What you need to do is find a way to convince others of your vision. With your very keen powers of observation and reason, it is not very hard at all for you to persuade others.

If there is a finance issue with a plan, invent a plan that circumvents that issue. Then present it. If you give a presentation to those who appear to have no interest in your ideas, you will get a better idea of what exactly interests them. Now, you may have some hesitation at the very thought of this. Perhaps you think you are bad at explaining your ideas to others. But giving a presentation is not the same as being a smooth talker. What's important is understand the feelings of the person you are presenting to. You just need to get them to listen. Picasso, Shigesato Itoi… These are some people born under the same star as you. They were also great presenters. You, too, have the same powers within you.

STARMAP
SCORPIO

9

Don't let your hobbies just be hobbies.

The world of instinct bubbles up within you, and Scorpios are intimately connected with it. This is because your star is Pluto. You have an unwavering core within you, and it leads you to be true to your instinct, and to throw yourself into wherever it leads you. The opinions of others are irrelevant. If you find something you think is important, that is enough for you.

When you cannot make things go as you desire them in your professional life, you have a tendency to say that "work is work" and throw all your remaining energy into your hobbies. And it's true that there is nothing wrong with that. But there is also no need to completely separate your hobbies from your job. If you like to work with your hands, to make little crafts and things, there may come a day when that skill will serve you in your professional life as well. If you are a history buff, perhaps you can find a way to make a name for your city, your area. When you are interested in something, you get serious about it and study up on it and absorb as much information as you can.

If you cut all that skill and information off from your professional life, then you will never get a chance to put it to use outside of your hobby. So make an effort to bridge your hobbies and work. This is not to say that your skills will immediately lead to work, but in the future you may open a store or start a business. When it comes time to stand on your own, those skills will help you. See to it that you connect your professional and recreational lives. It will expand horizons and fill your life with ever more possibility.

STARMAP
SCORPIO

10

Prepare, observe.

You're unmotivated at work. You don't even care about your hobbies or the other things that used to bring you joy. There are people who, when they feel that way, rush to do something, anything, and haphazardly rush to action. But you, Scorpio, are better off pausing, and taking the time to observe your surroundings. Just as the scorpion buries in the sand and waits for his prey, the longer you observe, the better your future will be.

You are not only intuitive, you are observant, and as you observe you'll come to see many things you were previously unable to. So just pause and observe the situation or person in question. Then you can think about what to do. You don't need to be on the front lines. Take a step back. If a fellow employee has messed up and is being disciplined by the boss, take a moment to observe the two of them. What kind of people are they? Why did the employee mess up? If you were in the boss' position, how would you respond? If there is trouble afoot, how would you deal with it?

Observe and simulate how you would react. Then, all the power and knowledge you've stored up will serve you well in the future when something bad does happen, or when your back is up against the wall. The chance to use your strengths will come, absolutely.

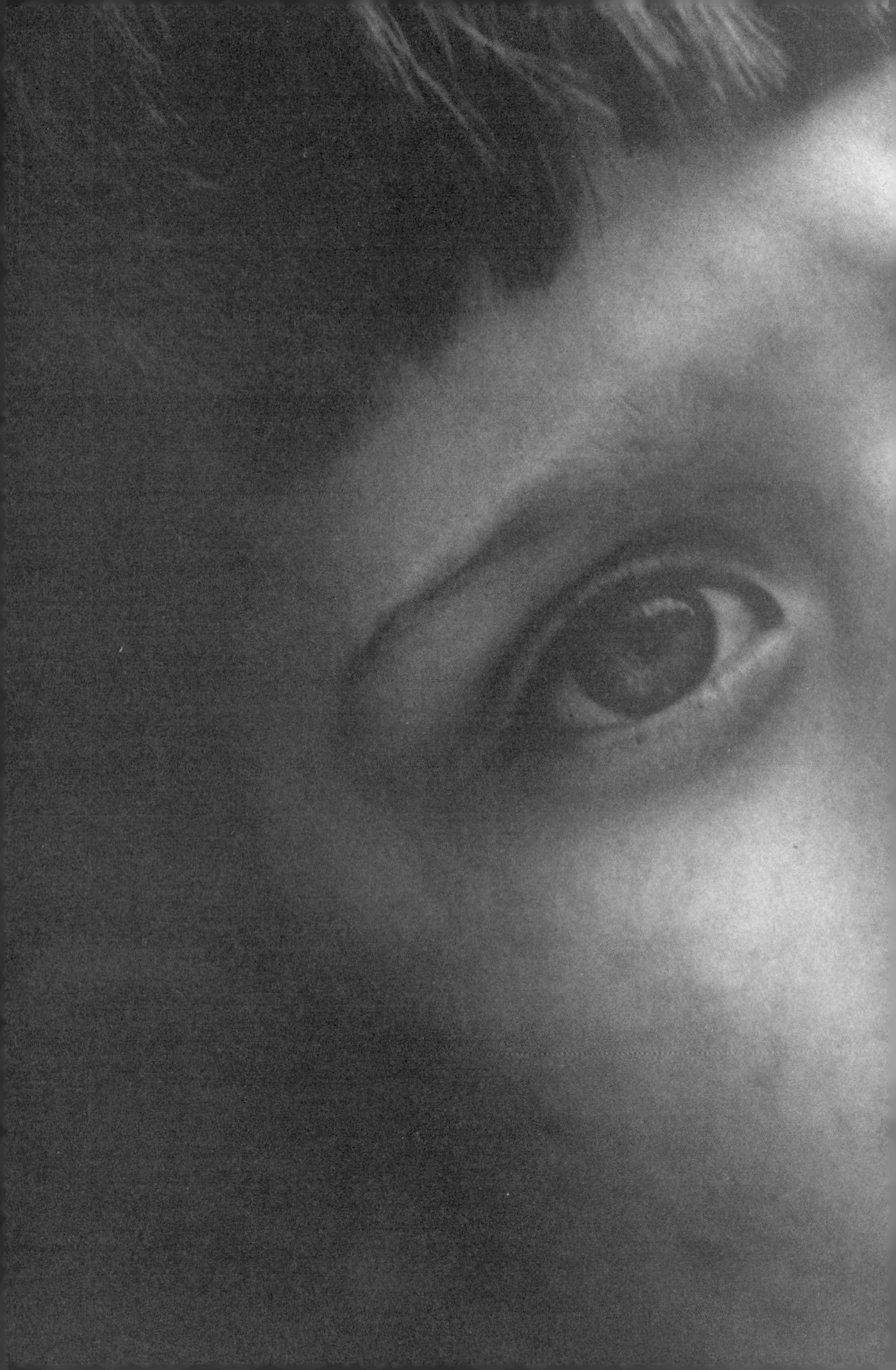

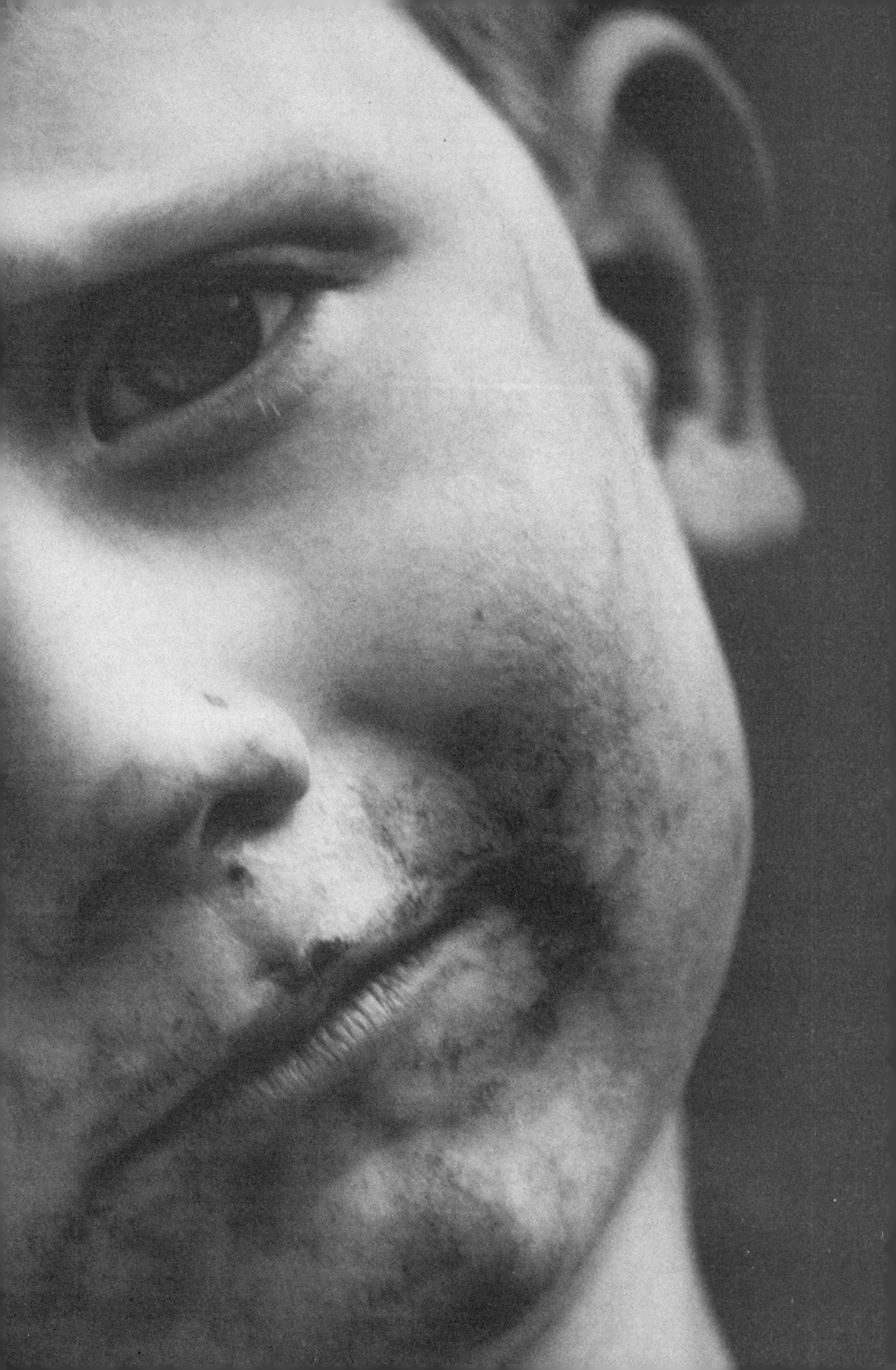

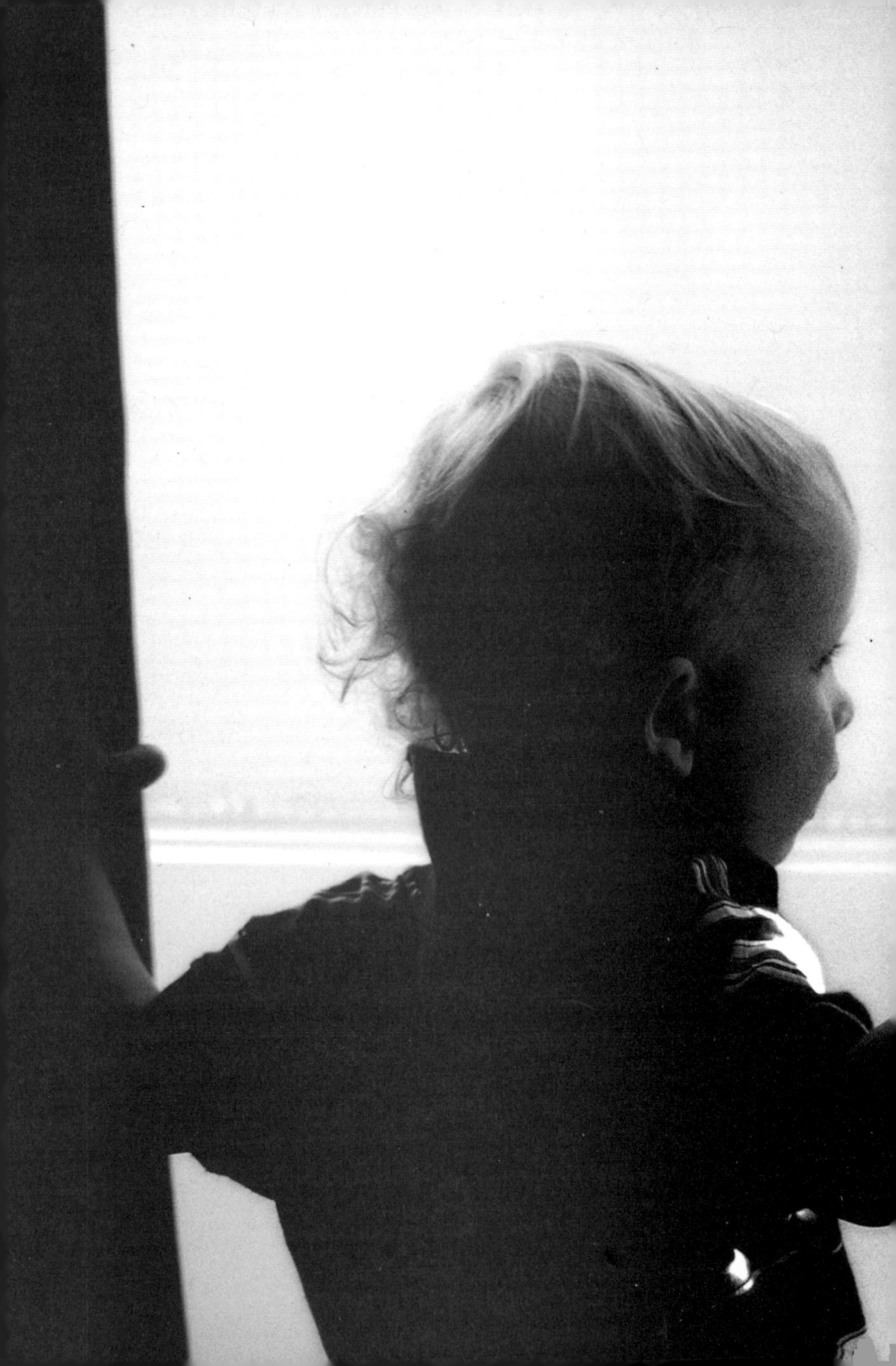

STARMAP SCORPIO

What to choose and why.

(Choices / Decisions)

Life is a series of choices.
You are the result of your past choices,
and your future self will be the result of choices you make now.
What should a Scorpio choose?
How should you decide?

STARMAP
SCORPIO

11

Focus on what you enjoy.

When most people are faced with large decisions, they consider what they like and dislike, the merits and demerits. But that is not how Scorpios makes up their minds. For example, even if 99% of the situation is full of demerits, that one percent that you like may be enough to convince you. You can fall in love with the value of that one percent, it can convince you to shoulder the burden of the other 99%. You can find a way to manage.

Others may watch you and say that you shouldn't make choices with a bias. But if you look at it objectively, Scorpios really make the best choices. Looking at the situation holistically may give one an idea of what is good and what is suitable, but these things change over time. What once seemed perfect and wonderful may, over time, lose its charm and come to mean nothing to you.

If you find something that you are sure of, something you know will never change, then it has a power over all the other detractors and issues. It has staying power. Artist and content-creators may only have one weapon in their arsenal, but it is a weapon that they can always use. You have a natural ability to see through the ephemeral to what will last. So even when it seems that something is covered in demerits, if you find something within it that is sure to last, don't hesitate. Go for it.

STARMAP
SCORPIO

12

Give yourself time to think.

You have things that are important to you, holy to you, and you often want to shut them up within. Scorpios, watched over by Pluto, often feel this way. Because you always make your own way and cut your own path, you will never be satisfied with your choices if they were made without consulting that voice deep within.

You are analytical, so you can acquire however much information you need without loosing your cool. But once you have all the information you need, you need to sink deep into your subconscious and listen to the voice speaking to you there. To do this, you need to have time. Ignore the information, turn off the TV, turn off the computer, take time to sit by yourself in your room and listen to what your heart is saying. Go out to the country where you can escape cell service for three days.

Avoid jumping to conclusions, and give yourself time to think. Until you make the time to have this conversation with your self, you will always wonder if you've made the right choices in life. Regret and doubt will follow you. To avoid those regrets, make the time to listen to the voice deep within your heart. It will tell you what you need to know. It will give you answers.

STARMAP
SCORPIO

13

Revisit the things you've given up on.

Even though you have let something go, Scorpios carry a little piece of their past experiences with them through life. They pull at you from behind. They are like little splinters in your heart. Most people don't look back on the things they've left behind. They feel little when they see those things. But Scorpios are different.

Even though you've given up on something, a little piece of it always seems to be stuck to you. You gave a great presentation, but failed to convince others, and your project never came to be. You'd always wanted to study overseas, but because of money and other issues, you were not able to. You started going to the gym, but you ran out of time and had to stop. There was someone you wanted to be friends with, wanted to grow closer to, but in the end they left school, or the company, and your relationship never came to be.

You may have given up on these things, but you did like them once, and they made you feel something. Those feelings revisit you. So it is important for Scorpios to revisit these past places. When you go back, you may find new things that you never noticed before. New angles of approach, new ways of thinking about things. It may bring new ideas to you. Revisit your past, and take a moment to pick up those things you've thrown away. You'll find new discoveries there.

**STARMAP
SCORPIO**

14

Look for deeper answers and find your true self.

You easily know when you like something. When you need to make a choice, it's best to rely on that feeling. But while you may like something superficially, on the surface of things, that doesn't mean that you really like it. Behind all of it lurks your real desires. It's important to you search for them. You may like a certain cafe because it's very fashionable and the coffee is good. But are those the real reasons? Could it be that you have a crush on the boy behind the counter? Or perhaps you like cafes and pubs, but don't like bars? Could it be that you just like places where groups of people gather? Look for the real reasons behind your emotions.

Furthermore, you may consider yourself sadistic. If that's so, look for a place where you can be masochistic for once. The surface and the depths. The light and shadow. Choose the opposite of your assumptions and you'll find answers there.

You may think yourself sadistic because you are always acting as sadistic as possible at work. But maybe you are masochistic in love? Or perhaps you are masochistic and, in order to hide it, you only pretend to be sadistic? Now think of something you despise. Do you really despise it? Take a good hard look at it. What makes you feel that way? Look for the real answers.

Perhaps you hate money because you can easily picture yourself drowning in it? Perhaps you cannot forgive infidelity because you secretly want to have relationships with all kinds of people? If you want to understand your true desires, look for the answers hiding behind your simple emotions.

STARMAP
SCORPIO

15

You don't need the
answers today.

When you make a choice, you may find others saying things like, "Why did you do that?," "You'll regret it," or "You'll never be happy that way." Pay them no heed. Don't look for the surface answers, look for the deeper meanings. That's just how Scorpios are.

You are not swayed by thoughts of profit or simple merits. What's important are your own values and whether or not something fits with them. You may not know the right answer today, or even tomorrow. The answers you are searching for may take five or ten years to come to you. But even if you make the wrong choice tomorrow, that's no reason to regret it. To push it even further, you may not have to make any decision at all.

Just let the current carry you where it will. If you decide to surrender yourself to the flow, it will certainly take you somewhere good. Just trust it. You do not need the understanding of others. You don't need to be immediately rewarded for you choices. Your choices are deeper than time, they are eternal.

**STARMAP
SCORPIO**

When you hit a wall, when you hit bottom.

(Adversity / Hard Times)

When do you really feel in trouble?
When you fail, when you hit a wall,
when you fall down…
It's okay.
You have your own way to turn things around.

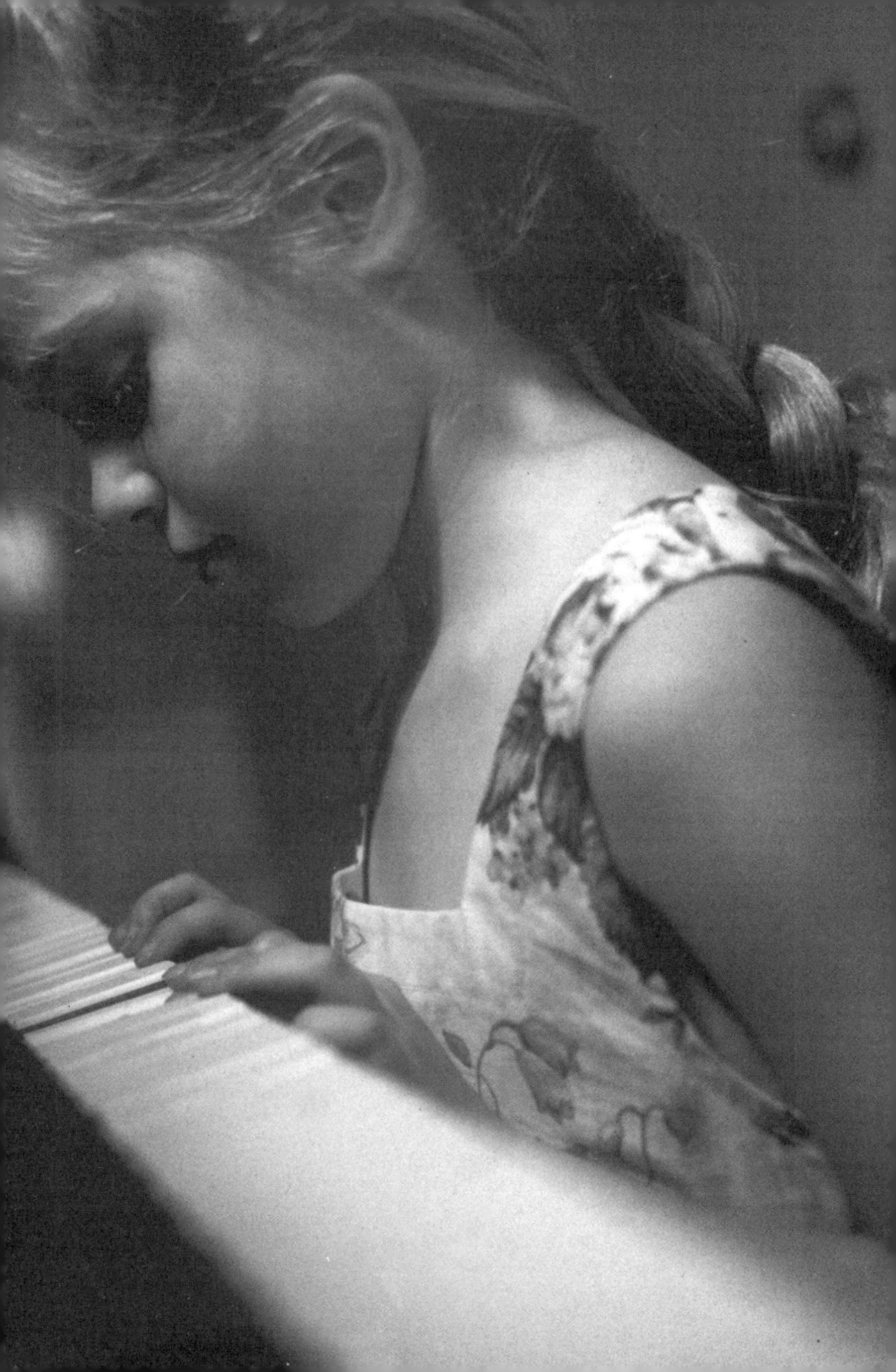

STARMAP
SCORPIO

16

You are strong when you're in a pinch.

Scorpios are often called fragile, delicate. And it may be true that your heart often moves in response to the littlest of things. But that doesn't mean that you are weak, or that you are afraid of trouble, pain, or fear. Tears may run down your face, but you are strong enough to stand your ground in any situation, and you are wise enough to grow from it.

You may be chased into a corner and run out of options, but in the process you learn what you really want from life. You might make a big mistake and be called out on it by everyone you know, but that gives you energy and drives you to change. You may have had your heart broken, but that is how you learn about pain and become nicer to others. That is how Scorpios are; they know how to turn negatives into positives.

This is why, when you are hurt or pushed into a corner, you don't need to get upset, you don't need to put your feelings out there for everyone to see. You have the ability to stay calm. You possess great self control. You may actually be hurt, but you don't want others to see how you feel, so you have a tendency to shut those feelings away in your heart. That puts others at ease, and people come from all around to depend on you. When they see you, calm and collected, dealing with an issue, you will earn everyone's respect.

You not only grow personally through your trials, but you also earn the respect of others, and it is in that way that you can turn a pinch into a chance. When you feel the pressure coming on, you can wield a power so great it will surprise even you.

STARMAP SCORPIO

17

It's okay to fail at something as long as you finish it.

Failure and loss are an inevitable part of life. But most people spend much of their life trying to avoid these very things. There are times when, halfway through something, it becomes apparent that the endeavor will end in failure. The majority of people give up at that point. They are afraid of failure and decide it is better to not continue at all. But it is better for a Scorpio to see it through. Because Scorpios tend to be a little stubborn, if you decide to just give up halfway through, the decision will haunt you and make it difficult to move on to the next step.

If you just rush into the next thing, you won't be able to devote your energies to it as you should. Therefore, if it seems as though you are going to fail at something, if there is 0% chance of success, it is still better for you to finish the project and see it through to the end. If it was a project you wanted to undertake in the beginning, don't give up at the first sign of failure. Experience the loss, experience the failure as deeply as you can. In sports, even if your team is beaten throughly, even if your rank falls drastically, play your best until the end. If you like someone and feel there is no chance they like you back, don't worry. Tell them how you feel and let them break your heart.

Once you realize how sorely you were beaten, once you realize that you tried your best but failed, that is when you will be able to move on to the next thing. There's no need to fear failure. Even if you know you won't succeed, go as far as you can and see it through to the end.

STARMAP
SCORPIO

18

Let things go.

Scorpio is the sign of water, and Scorpios are very sensitive to the emotions of others. This is true of negative emotions as well, so when you feel something unpleasant, or when you run up against a wall, you tend to fall to pieces. But Scorpios are also tough in a crisis, and so they meet the emotions head on, which causes more pain and stress. It leads to a negative spiral.

Realize that, no matter how stubborn or persistent you may be, there are always going to be issues that you simply cannot solve. Learn to let things go. Perhaps your boss keeps saying awful things, perhaps it's an awful job. Regardless, just let it go by. You might be given a terrible job, you might hit a thick wall...don't mind the frustration. Just focus on what you want to do, focus on what you can do, what you love. That thing might have heavy responsibilities, it might seem difficult. But Scorpios can do it.

When you let yourself become completely absorbed in something your head will clear. So when you hit a wall and are stressed by it, just focus on what you want to do instead. If you ignore and avoid the things you dislike, others may say you are unbalanced or selfish. But if you focus on what you love and do it with all your heart, you'll earn their respect in the end. The things you avoid to focus on other things may well solve themselves with time, and simpler ways to approach the issues may present themselves to you.

STARMAP
SCORPIO

19

Leave revenge to your imagination.

You may learn to let things go, but there are sometimes walls so large and problems to tenacious that they take hold of your mind and just won't let go. Once the negativity has overtaken you, it just won't leave you alone. Once you find yourself in a situation like that, it will creep into your subconscious and begin to influence your behavior and desicions. If you let it go unchecked for too long it may lead to secret plots of revenge. You must be careful not to let this happen.

One method is to let yourself go as far as your imagination will take you, as long as it is only in you imagination. There may be times when you don't know what to do in reality, but you can imagine things to be however you wish them to be. You can rid yourself of negativity by letting your imagination sink deeply into it.

Perhaps someone has betayed you and you are unable to forgive them. You take revenge on them in your imagination. Imagine whatever it is that you wish to do. If there is something preventing you from doing something you'd like to, imagine yourself breaking down that wall in whatever way you chose.

If you don't imagine it fully, it will have no effect on your actual life. You need to picture it so perfectly and thoroughly that you can actually feel it happening. Then your emotions will move in response to it; it will be as if you have actually rid yourself of those negative emotions. It will allow you to move on. You were born under the star of transformation, you can be reborn over and over again. If you allow yourself to imagine the banishment of those negative emotions, you can create an opportunity for rebirth within yourself.

STARMAP SCORPIO

20

You don't have to get rid of your negative emotions.

You can see things through to the end, you can ignore them, you can finish them in your imagination. There are many ways to recover once you have fallen. So there is always some way to stand up and brush yourself off. But there is always a chance that some of that negativity will stay with you. You may not have rid yourself of it completely.

There is no way to say that your negative emotions of loss, discouragement, or betrayal will vanish for good. You hold on to emotions in a deeper way than others do. You may think you have forgotten someone, when a sudden memory of their face comes back to you and your heart reacts. There is nothing wrong with that. As long as people are people, their hearts are sure to contain some measure of sadness and pain and envy.

You are able to be yourself because of those very emotions. So take all of it and store it away within your heat. If you do, then that pain will someday change into nourishment, it will cause you to grow. It will form a wellspring. With all your resources at hand, you are sure to grow newer and ever more beautiful.

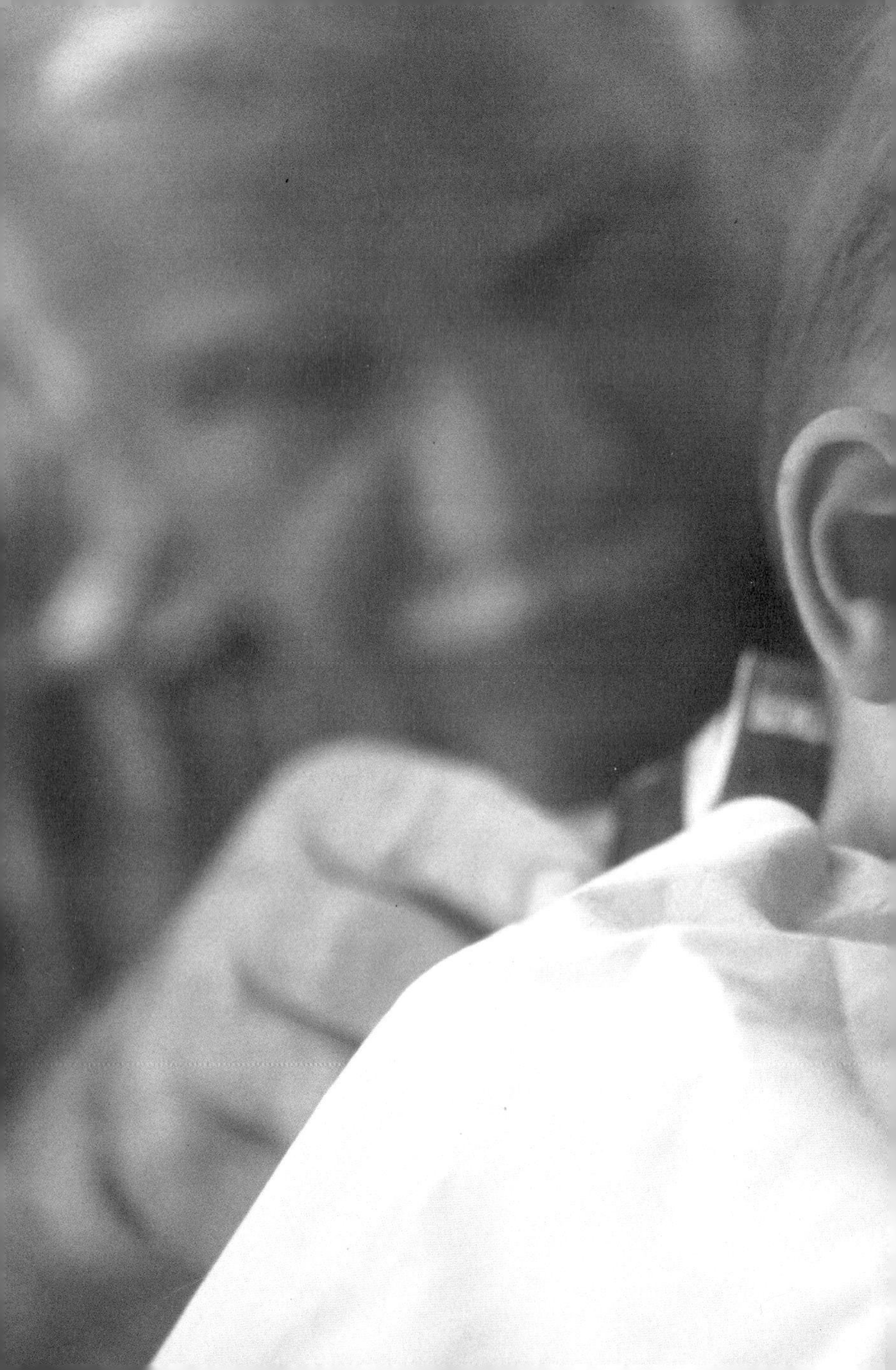

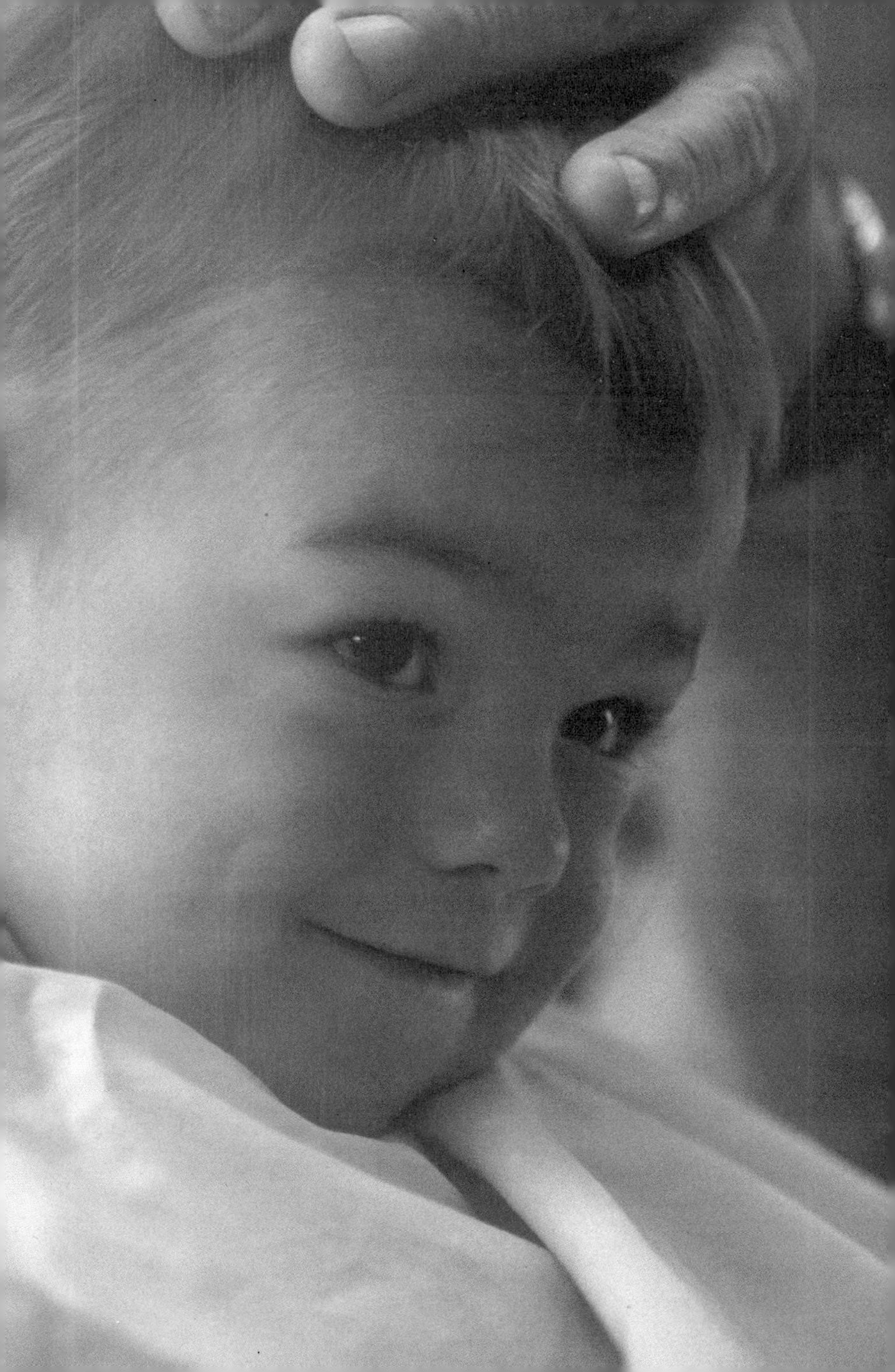

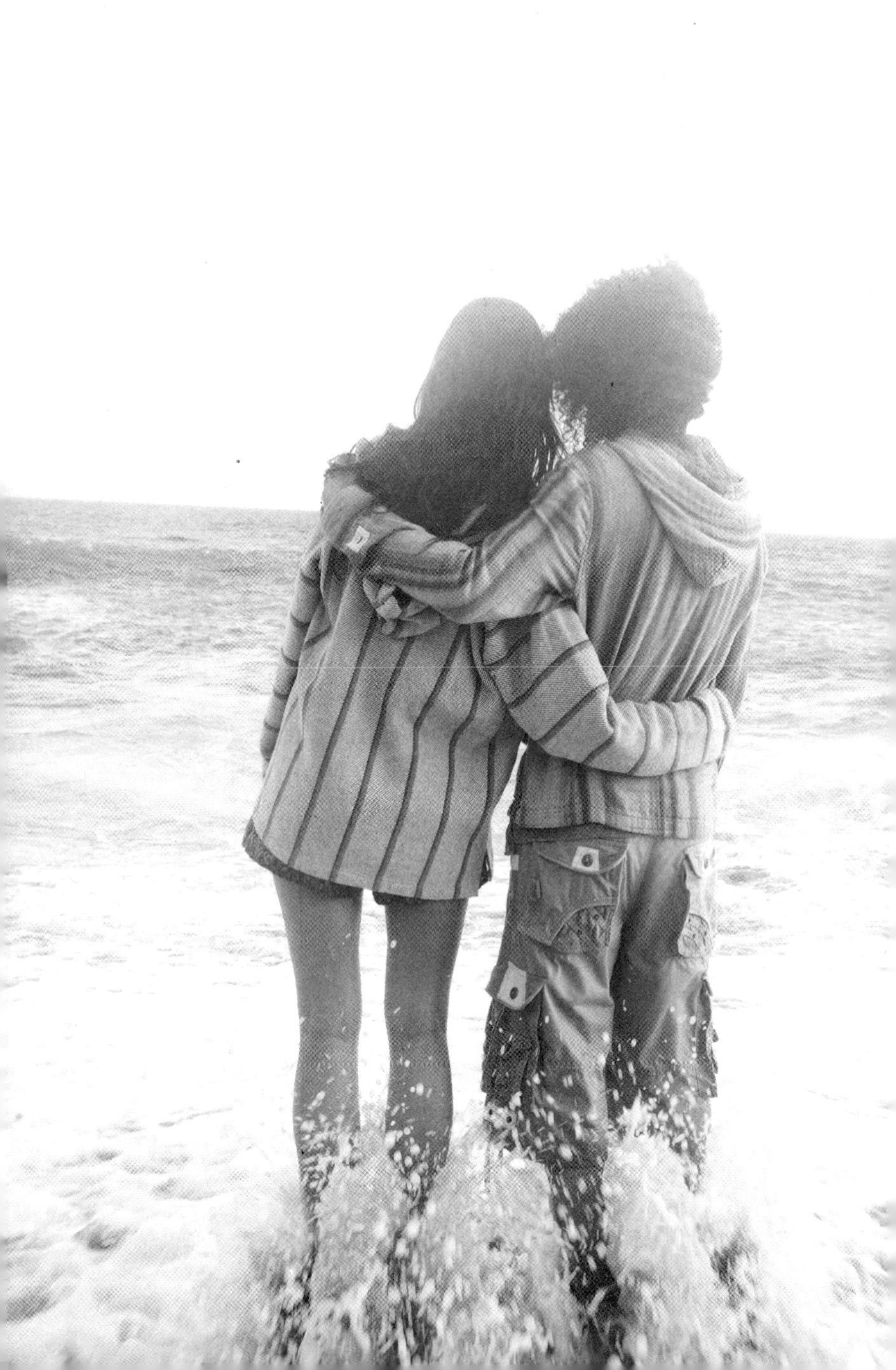

**STARMAP
SCORPIO**

Who will you love?
Who will love you?

(Personal Relationships / Love)

What kind of person should you love?
Who will really understand you?
Who will allow you to be more like yourself?
Who will allow you to grow?
How do you form deeper relationships?

STARMAP
SCORPIO

21

Have the courage to take the first step.

You want to become one with another person, to forget the boundaries of self. You want them to accept you completely. You also want to completely accept them. But at the same time you are afraid of having a deep relationship with another person. You feel this way because you have been hurt in the past. You might be interested in someone, find them attractive, but unable to take the first step.

Psycologists call this the "Hedgehog's dilemma." Two hedgehogs want to grow close to one another, but as they do they injure one another with their spines. You, too, are afraid of pain, and therefore you are afraid to take the first step. Yet you still wish to have a deep relationship with another. You try to have distance with many people in your life, but that puts more pressure on your partner to fill your emotional needs, and you end up getting hurt because of it.

You may have had traumatic experiences in the past because of this. To counter this, try not to put all your needs on one person. Try to have meaningful relationships with all the people in your life. If you are interested in ten people, send out an email to all of them. Invite them out to dinner, take the first step. If you do, then each step accomplishes more, and you don't need to completely depend on one other person. Don't create relationships to fill the holes in your own self, create them to have real connections with others. Don't worry: if you are interested in someone, take the first step.

STARMAP
SCORPIO

22

Become someone your partner needs.

The amount of energy you give to others is astonishing. You want to become one with them. That energy helps you to build deep relationships, but it can also be the cause of desire, anger, and jealousy. This is because you want to hold on to your partner in the deepest, most meaningful way you can. If that energy is causing you trouble, stop giving it to others. Use it on yourself.

Scorpios are often compared to the high-flying eagle because of their powers of perception. You know what your partner wants even before they do, and you swoop in ahead in time to provide it. When your company is busy you can tell what data is needed, and you prepare it before it is even requested. If your partner is worried about their health, you cook only the healthiest foods for them.

As you perform these tasks, others come to depend on you at work, privately, and in love. You become irreplaceable. Once you see that happening, you will gain confidence, and your anger and jealousy will dissipate. It will be easy to form lasting relationships.

Scorpios can expose themselves completely if it means forming a real bond with someone. That doesn't mean that you lose yourself, rather, that you find yourself in the actions you perform for others. When you feel needed and form a real, deep connection with someone, your heart will fill to the brim with happiness.

STARMAP
SCORPIO

23

Who should you love?

Scorpios take time to really open themselves up to another person. You have a place inside yourself that you are hesitant to allow another into. It is because you know of these places that you respect the boundaries of others. If your partner is as sensitive of a person as you are, then it may take time for the both of you to open up, but once you do, the bond you form will be very, very deep.

If you meet someone who seems simplistic, someone who moves forward through life with incredible momentum, if you meet someone like that, you might consider giving yourself over to their inertia. If you've been with them long enough to see that you get along, they'll be able to relax all those emotions you've kept pent up inside.

So, what of those people that seem relaxed all the time? While you try so hard at all you do, struggle with your passions, haven't you ever felt drawn to those relaxed individuals that just do whatever they feel like? If you allow yourself to be with someone like that, you'll learn to see simple pleasures in life. Your tenacity and effort are what make you the great person you are, but don't try too hard. It's alright for you to relax and have fun. It's alright to have fun. Soon you'll find yourself more relaxed, more joyful, than you were before.

STARMAP
SCORPIO

24

Who will really love you?

Scorpios are filled with violent energy and emotion. You are aware of that, and not wanting others to find you "obnoxious" or "dramatic," you often try to maintain a little distance between your true self and others. But the person who is right for you will accept your intensity. If you are courageous and take the first step, they are sure to accept, even rejoice in, the strength of your heart and the seriousness of your thoughts.

It's not only your intensity; it's your weakness, fragility, pain, wounded heart...they'll accept it all. Even the things you didn't know you had contained within yourself. There is no need to pry the doors of your heart open. They will open with time. If you have someone who will love you for who you are, then there is no need for you to fear, no need to rush or to doubt. They will accept all of it. So don't be afraid; believe.

Deep in your heart is a lake, or a well. The bottom of it is lined with treasures that not even you are aware of. Someone who loves you can see to the bottom, see your thoughts, find those treasures, and protect them. When someone who loves you believes in you, you'll discover things about yourself you never knew. You'll meet the real you.

STARMAP SCORPIO

25

Breaking up is not the end, it will bring you new possibilities.

Break ups. They are an inevitable part of life. They are hard, especially for Scorpios, who love with all their hearts, put themselves out there, and try to be one with another. It feels like the ground is breaking away from under you. But there is a talent there, hidden in the pain. It shows how deeply you can feel. The emotion might be negative, but your emotions are still filled with power. That power will help you grow; it will pull you into the future.

There are people who, faced with a loss and desperate to run from their negative feelings, will rush into relationships with people they feel nothing for. There are people who will drown themselves in alcohol. There are people who will chase after the person that hurt them, ruining any chance or reconciliation in the process. But none of these coping mechanisms are for you. This is not to say that you should throw away your feelings and move on. Face your sadness head on, hold tight to that hole left by a lost love. Cry it out. It is hard to feel sadness that seems to have no end. But you don't need to see the end of it. If you face it and cry it out, the end will come.

At the end there will be new people and new experiences waiting for you. Scorpios are based on the water animal, the scorpion, but often they grow wings and fly through the air like an eagle. They are also called the snake and and are associated with alchemy. All these forms are because you were born under the star of transformation. But in order to be reborn, you first have to die. Once you die and overcome your sadness, you'll come back immortal, a phoenix.

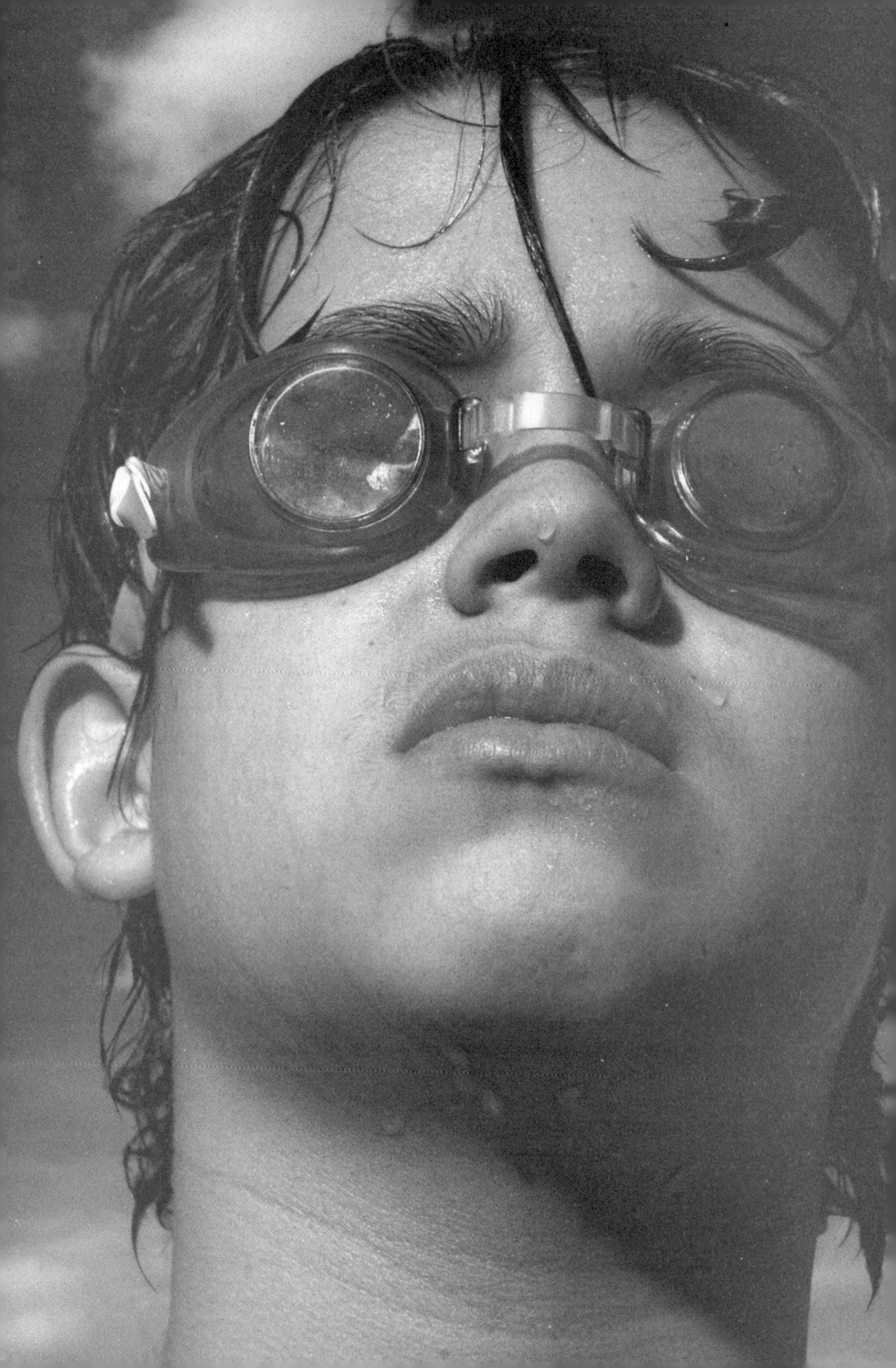

STARMAP SCORPIO

What to value.

How to be yourself.

(Rules / Desires)

What does it mean to be yourself?
Everyone is born with individualism.
But in the process of growing up,
have you lost sight of it?
What must you do to recover it?

STARMAP
SCORPIO

26

Flexibility, not flattery.

Scorpios have an unwavering core within them. They are not swayed by the opinions of others, they know very well what they like and dislike. That doesn't necessarily mean that you are prideful or incapable of compromise. When you meet something that is truly worth your time, you can easily throw aside your pride and give your heart to it. Therefore there is no need to flatter others.

Stay true to your own values. In order to do so, try to shut out as much outside information as you can. Set aside your phone, turn off the computer, and give your thoughts time to mature. That is the best life for you. The only thing you must be aware of is this: Others depend on you more than you might think. You may not go out of your way to force your values on others, but even without doing so, by means of your mysterious power, others are drawn to you. Because of this, staying true to your own ideals may occasionally cause pain to others.

Try to carry a cushion, one with which you soften the blows, one with which you accept the words of others. There is no need to submit to, to accept, the values of others. Accept what they say with flexibility and discover where it relates to your own value system. If you do so, more and more people will come to understand who you really are, and opportunities for growth will present themselves more often.

STARMAP
SCORPIO

27

Be aware of your own darkness.

The times would have one think that we must be happy and bright all the times. But Scorpios' hearts are not only filled with positivity and joy. No, there are shadows in there, darkness in there, difficult emotions with which you grapple. Dostoevsky speaks of "Crime and punishment." Stevenson speaks of "Dr. Jekyll and Mr. Hyde." Scorpios produce much art, all of it aware of the true nature of our hearts. How is one to approach their own darkness and pain?

The method you chose will have a deep impact on your life. It is the key to your growth and happiness. If you ignore the darkness within, then before you notice, it will grow, reach out, and take you over. Don't ignore it; face it, stare it down. You don't need to pretend it isn't there, you only need to discover the source of it.

If you face your dark side, you'll learn to control it, and your powers of observation will grow ever sharper. It will lend you respect and kindness. You will understand others more than you did before. There is no need to appear as a "good person" or a "fun person." It is better, then, to value your darkness, your hatred and jealously, better then to learn how to best cope with it. Once you learn to do so, you'll become more attractive to others, and you'll grow into a better, wiser person.

STARMAP
SCORPIO

28

Focus on what you love and cross all borders.

When a Scorpio gets serious about something, they command powers of concentration the rest of the world lacks. They invest themselves fully into it, forgetting to eat or drink, and no matter the difficulty or annoyance of the job, a Scorpio doesn't care. Before you know it, Scorpios command deep knowledge and technique. So when you find something you love, allow yourself to lose yourself in it and continue on. If there are books you like, go ahead and read 100 of them in a month. If you like paintings, try to create so many of them you cover all the walls in your house. If you like to ride bicycles, why not bike across the country? If you like to bake, stay up all night and make as many types of cake as you can manage.

Do more than what is normal, more than you would think you were capable of. You'll fall into what athletes call "the zone", a trance-like state where your skills and talents push you over whatever borders you thought were there. These successes will help you grow and deepen your interpersonal relationships.

If you were to read a lot of books, not only do you gain knowledge about the books themselves, but your wisdom and concentration increase as well. If you ride a bike across the country, you'll meet a lot of people in the process, and become a better communicator. Even more important than these things, however, is the confidence you will gain in the process. You have the ability to lose yourself in what you love. Believe in it, and follow it where it takes you.

STARMAP
SCORPIO

29

To be reborn, experience all you can.

Everyone, throughout their lives, dies and is reborn many times. Like an insect shedding it's shell, you throw away your old self and re-emerge, fresh and new. Scorpios go through this process more dramatically than anyone else. There are times in your life when you change so rapidly that it seems to others that a new person is standing where you once were. That is growth, and it will always lead you in a good direction.

Well, then, what exactly brings about these moments of transformation? Experiences. As I've said throughout this book, it is those meetings that touch your heart and move your soul. It is those people you want to become one with. Experiences like that will inspire you to throw away your own shell. That is how you grow.

But Scorpios are true to their own ideals, they don't often show their true selves to others, and therefore, their opportunities for transformation are not as plentiful as others. A few times in your life, perhaps. There are people who only experience this once. But when you are given the chance, you can change more than others, and you can grow more. To facilitate this, open yourself up, meet as many people as you can. The more people you meet, the more opportunities you'll have to move your heart. And when it moves, you'll feel cracks form in your shell. You're on your way to your new self.

STARMAP
SCORPIO

30

Meeting people will help you meet your dreams.

What is a Scorpio's highest goal? A job they can lose themselves in. A hobby they are obsessive about. These things will certainly bring you satisfaction. But they are not what you long for the most. What you really desire is deep and lasting relationships with others. You want to become with someone you love and admire. When you truly fall in love, you will put aside your job and hobbies, even your dreams, to pursue it.

Others may say that you are dependent upon your love, or that you're obsessive. Pay them no heed. A Scorpio's need to connect with others is not the same as dependence. Experiencing new value systems is what will help you grow. That is what you desire. All of your encounters, all the people you meet, they set off a process in you like a chemical reaction.

That person you love, that person who moves you, who you've made a deep connection with, someday that person will share your dream, they will help you to chase it. They will help you search for the treasures buried deep in your heart. Therefore, there is nothing more important for you than the connections you form with others. If you value those connections, they will lead you to your dream.

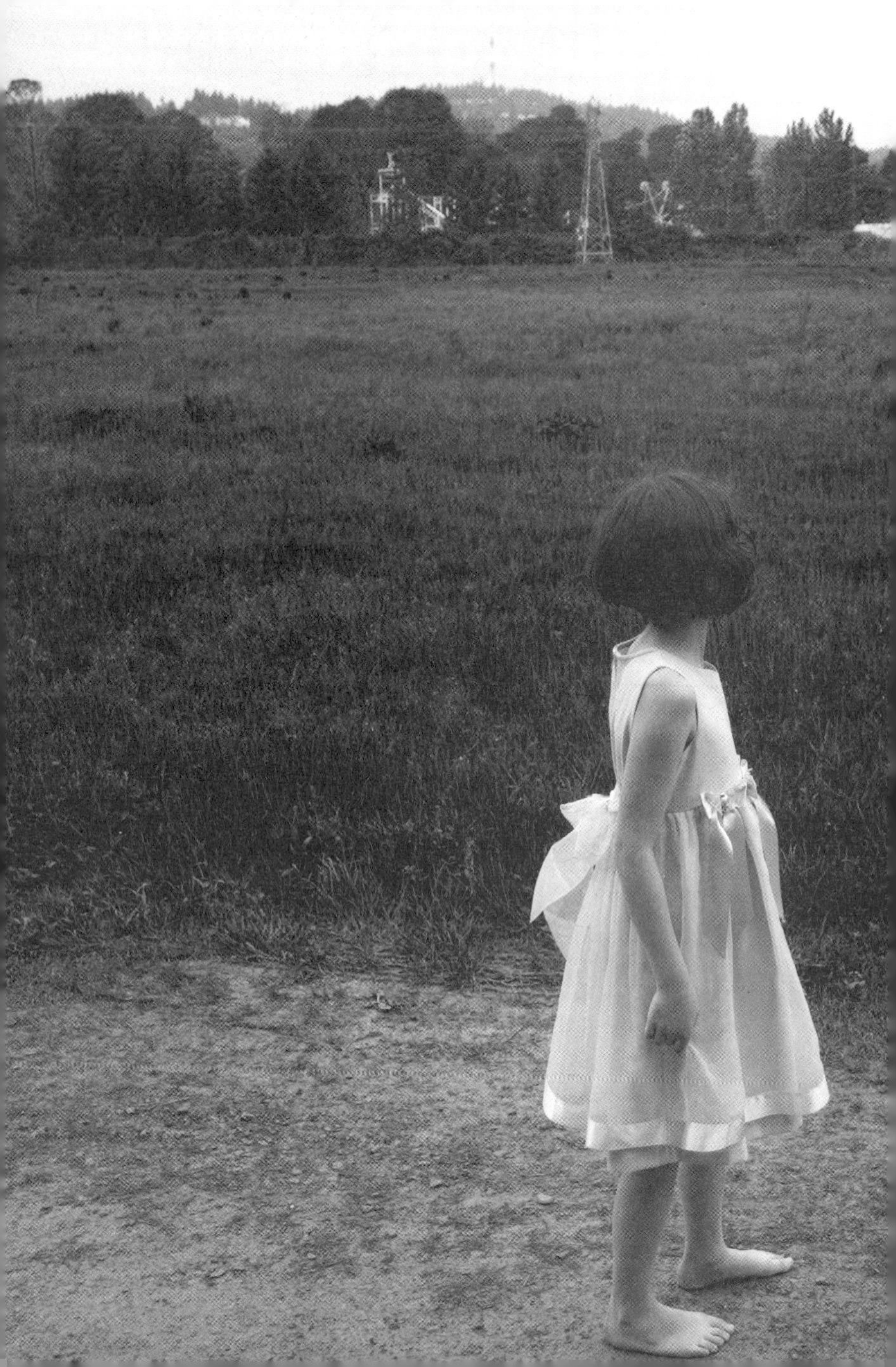

STARMAP
SCORPIO

To live without regret.

(Epilogue)

What does it mean to live?
To make your future shine brighter,
to bring more wealth to your life,
what do you need to live without regret?

**STARMAP
SCORPIO**

31

You are reborn time after time.

There is a power that sleeps
within you.
You may have not ever seen it.
When it moves you, it will surprise
even you.

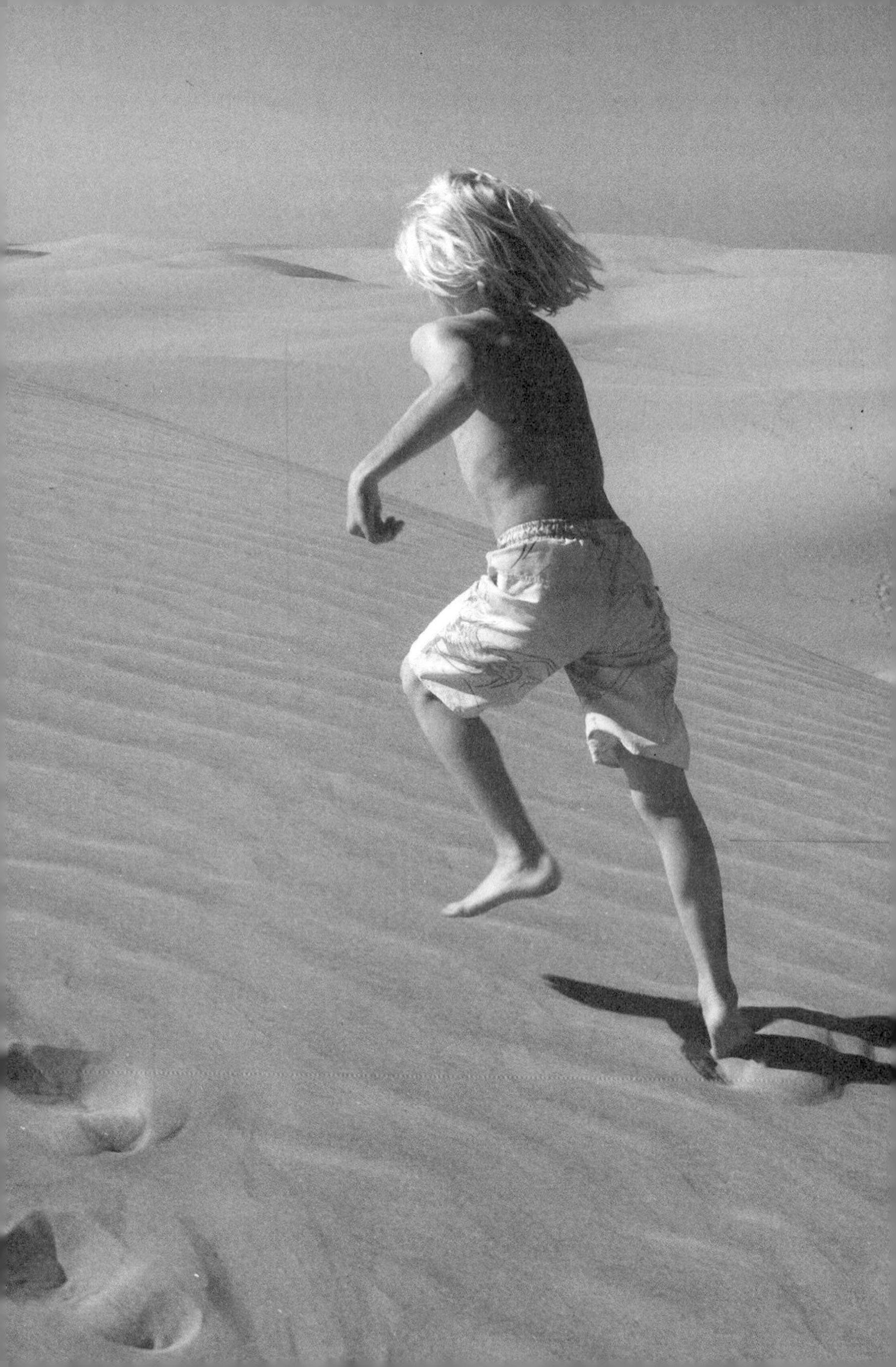

Life is not a gentle path with no detours.
There are places you cannot pass without taking a sudden leap.
There are many times in the life of a Scorpio that require your rebirth.

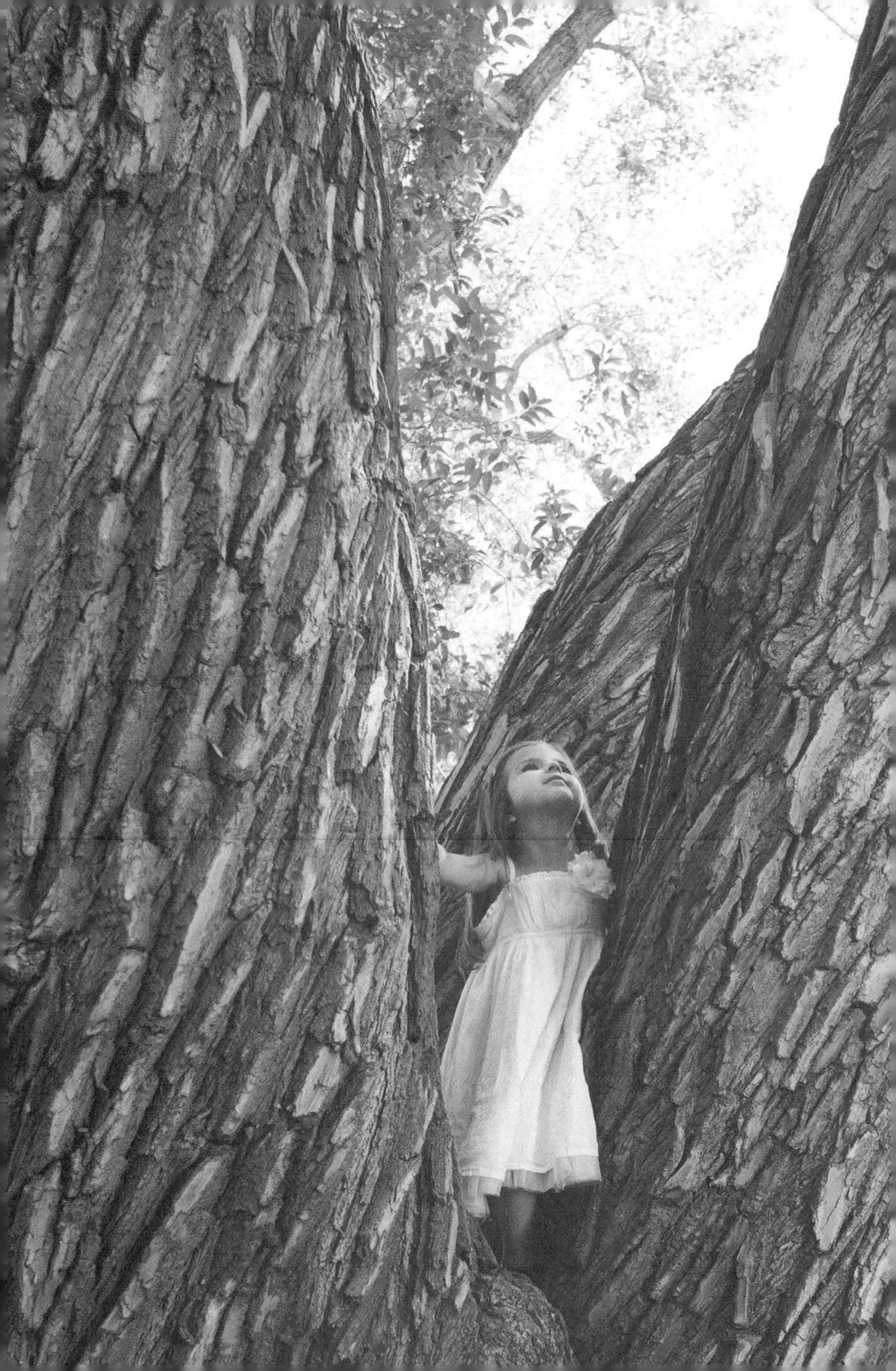

But there is no need to fear.

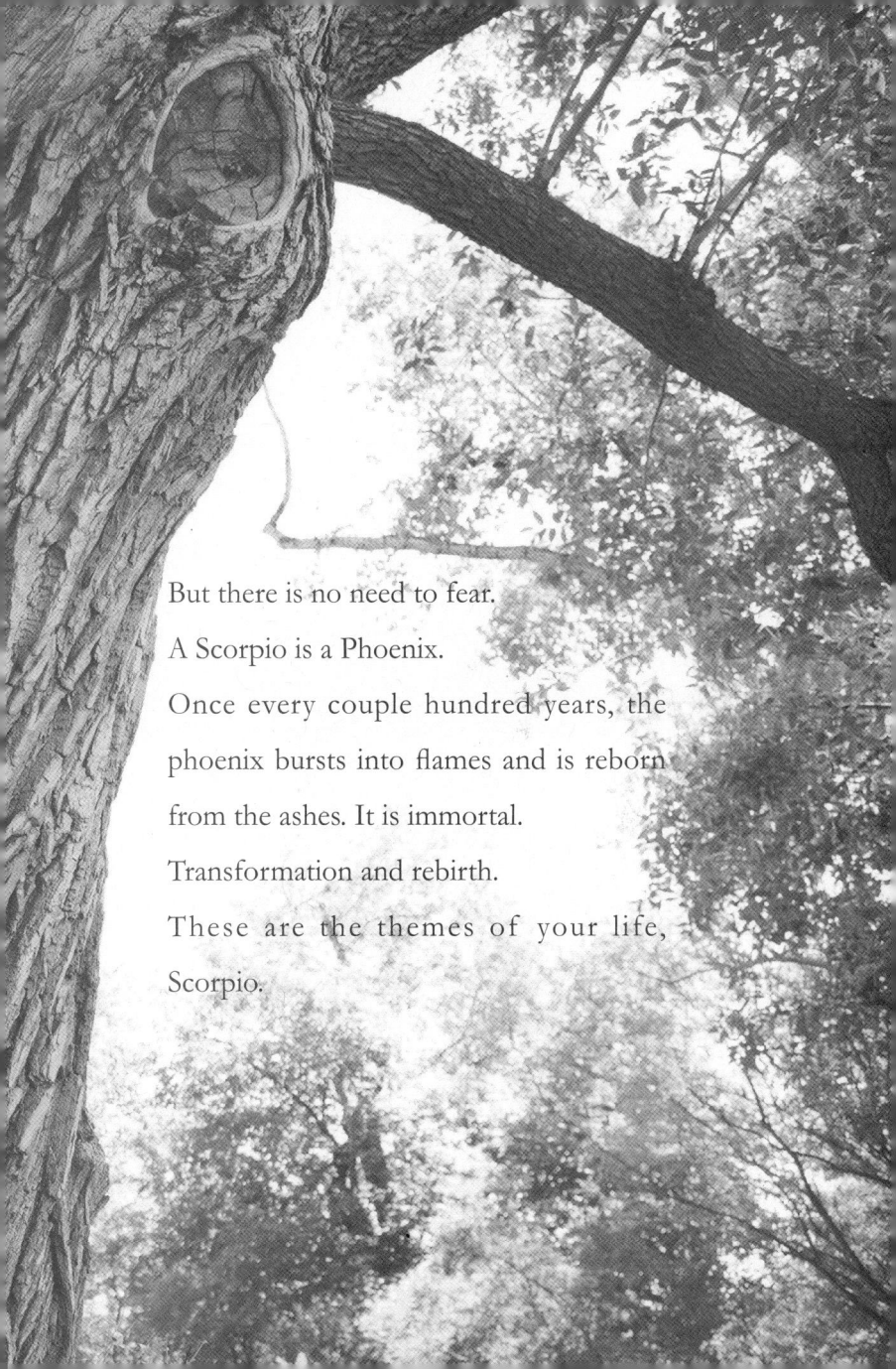

A Scorpio is a Phoenix.

Once every couple hundred years, the phoenix bursts into flames and is reborn from the ashes. It is immortal.

Transformation and rebirth.

These are the themes of your life, Scorpio.

You can cross any border.

You are not afraid of being swallowed by the waves.

You have the willpower to see things to their end.

And you will meet others.

You will meet a new you as well.

You didn't throw away your old self.

You grew wings, and you see from a higher vantage point.

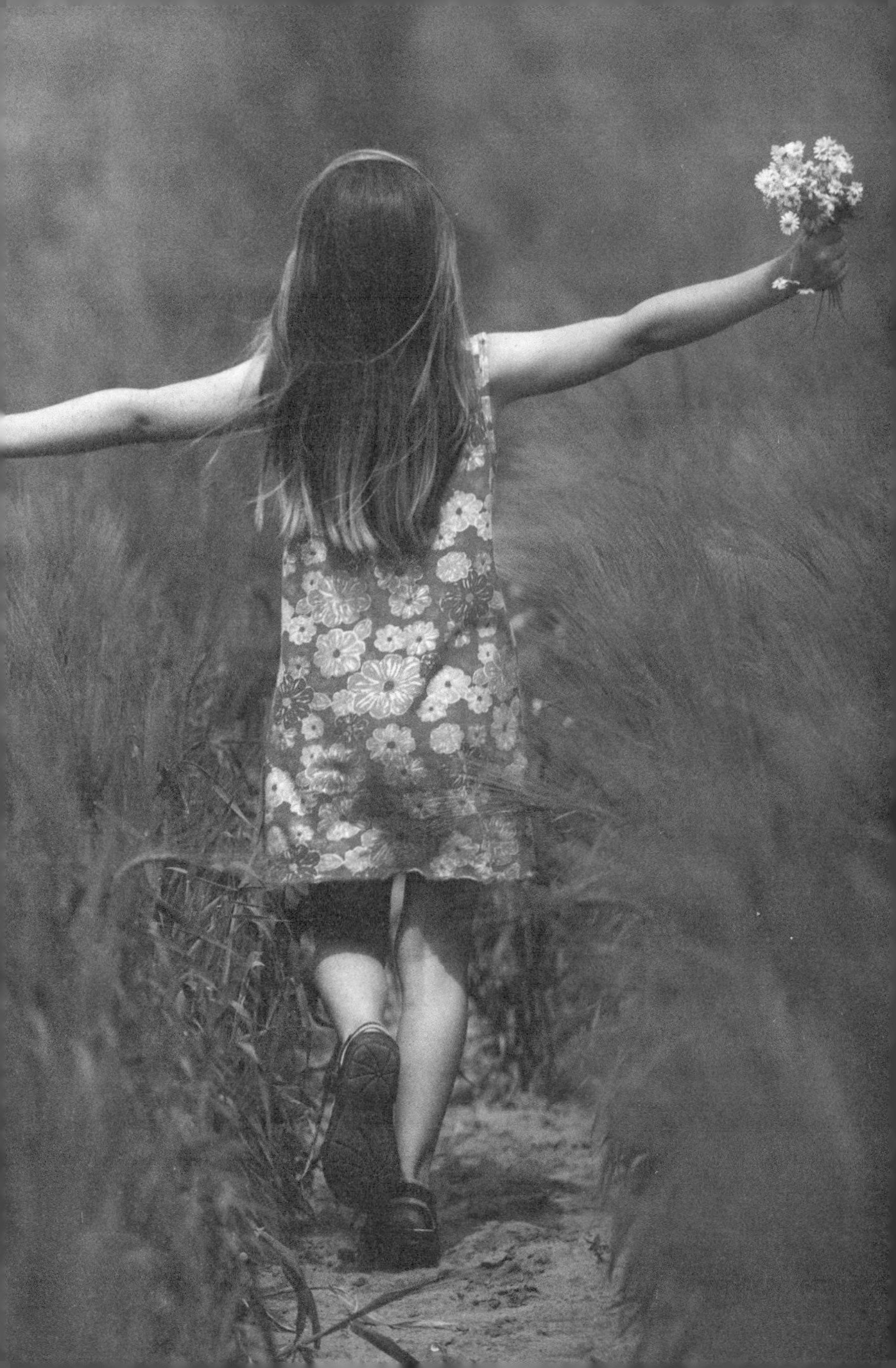

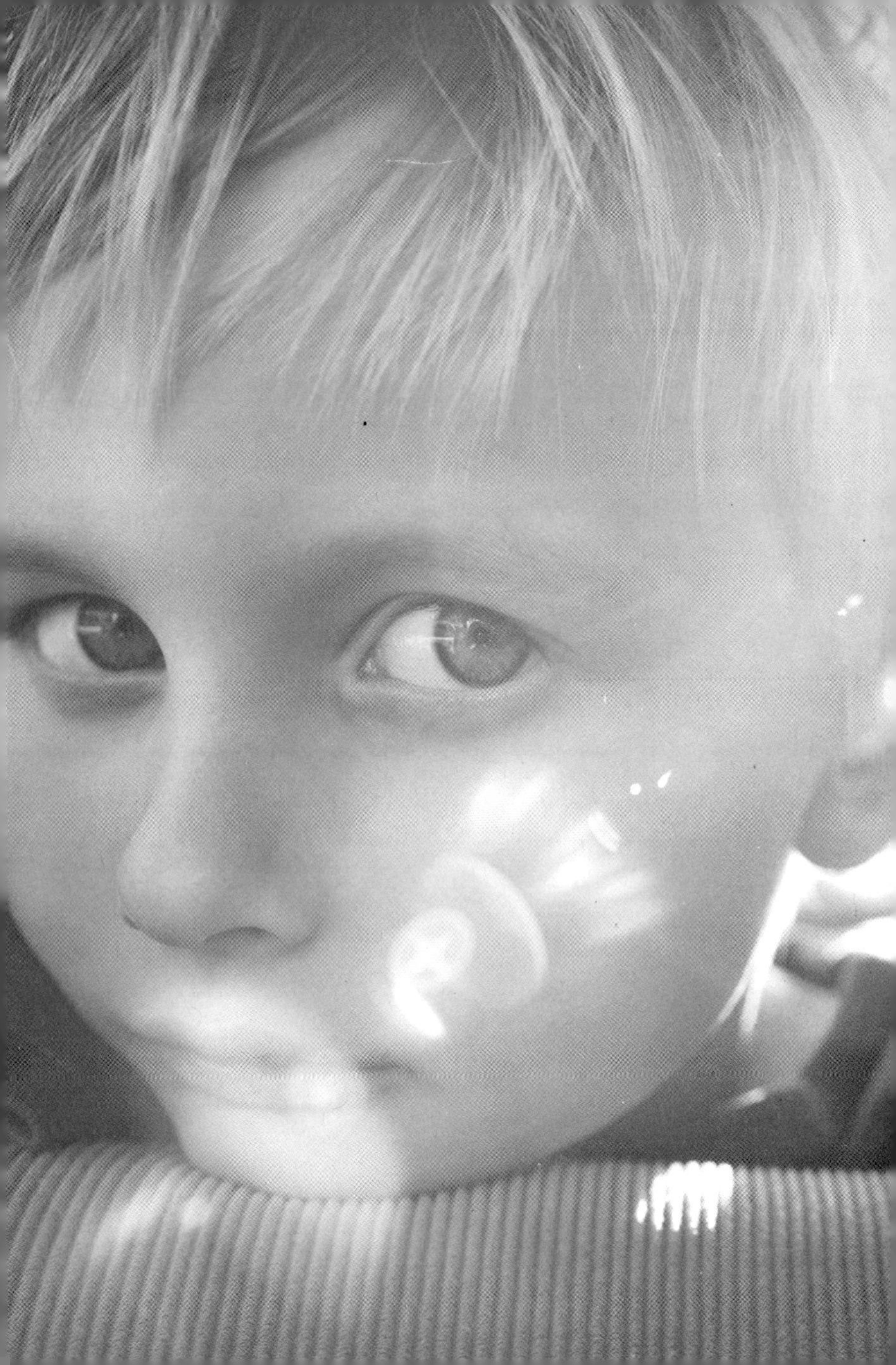

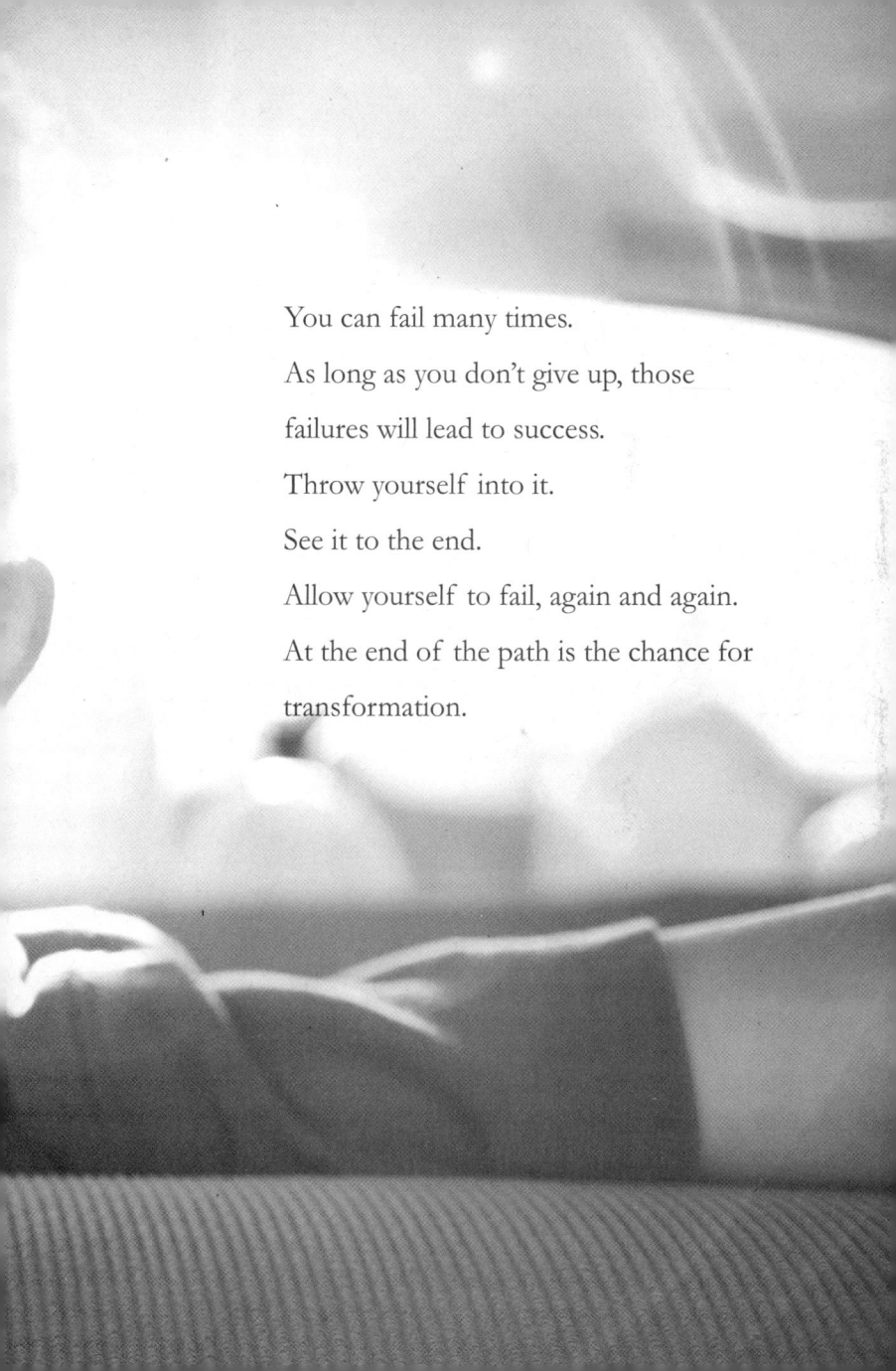

You can fail many times.
As long as you don't give up, those
failures will lead to success.
Throw yourself into it.
See it to the end.
Allow yourself to fail, again and again.
At the end of the path is the chance for
transformation.

You are reborn time and again.
Time and again.

Ryuji Kagami

Ryuji Kagami was born in 1968 in Kyoto, Japan. He began writing on astrological topics in his teens, where he became a local sensation. After graduating from university he quickly achieved national prominence, and now is a celebrity in Japan, known for his accurate readings and translations of important astrological texts. He is a member of the Association of Professional Astrologers International (APAI). Aside from writing books on the zodiac signs and tarot cards, Kagami keeps himself busy with blogs, radio, and television performances. This series of books on the zodiac signs marks his North American publishing debut.

STARMAP
SCORPIO

Scorpio

Copyright text © 2014 Ryuji Kagami
Copyright images © cobis/amana images

ISBN 978-1-935548-63-8

No part of this may be reproduced or transmitted in any form or by any means, electronic or mechanical, including photocopying, recording, or by storage and retrieval system without the written permission from the publisher. For more information contact One Peace Books.

Published by One Peace Books, Inc. in 2014
Cover and interior design by Shimpachi Inoue
Special thanks to Hoshiyomi Bunko

One Peace Books
43-32 22nd Street #204 Long Island City, NY 11101 USA
www.onepeacebooks.com

Printed in Canada